Napoleon's Campaign in Russia 1812

Napoleon's Campaign in Russia 1812

An Analysis of the French Campaign From
a Logistical and Medical Perspective

Achilles Rose

LEONAUR

Napoleon's Campaign in Russia 1812
An Analysis of the French Campaign From a Logistical and Medical Perspective
by Achilles Rose

First published under the title
Napoleon's Campaign in Russia Anno 1812

Leonaur is an imprint of Oakpast Ltd

Copyright in this form © 2012 Oakpast Ltd

ISBN: 978-0-85706-990-0 (hardcover)
ISBN: 978-0-85706-991-7 (softcover)

http://www.leonaur.com

Publisher's Notes

Contents

CENTRAL RUSSIA
THE WAR OF 1812

English Miles

Preface

There is no campaign in the history of the world which has left such a deep impression upon the heart of the people than that of Napoleon in Russia, 1812.

Of the soldiers of other wars who had not come home it was reported where they had ended on the field of honour. Of the great majority of the 600 thousand who had crossed the Niemen in the month of June 1812, there was recorded in the list of their regiments, in the archives *"Disappeared during the Retreat"* and nothing else.

When the few who had come home, those hollow eyed spectres with their frozen hands, were asked about these comrades who had disappeared during the retreat, they could give no information, but they would speak of endless, of never-heard-of sufferings in the icy deserts of the north, of the cruelty of the Cossacks, of the atrocious acts of the Moushiks and the peasants of Lithuania, and, worst of all, of the infernal acts of the people of Wilna. And it would break the heart of those who listened to them.

There is a medical history of the hundreds of thousands who have perished during 1812 in Russia from cold, hunger, fatigue or misery.

Such medical history cannot be intelligible without some details of the history of events causing and surrounding the deaths from cold and hunger and fatigue. And such a history I have attempted to write.

Casting a glance on the map on which the battlefields on the march to and from Moscow are marked, we notice that it was not a deep thrust which the attack of the French army had made into the colossus of Russia. From the Niemen to Mohilew, Ostrowno, Polotsk, Krasnoi, the first time, Smolensk, Walutina, Borodino, Conflagration of Moscow, and on the retreat the Battles of Winkonow, Jaroslawetz, Wiasma, Vop, Krasnoi, the second time, Beresina, Wilna, Kowno; this is not a great distance, says Paul Holzhausen in his book *Die Deutschen in*

Russland 1812 but a great piece of history.

Holzhausen, whose book has furnished the most valuable material of which I could avail myself besides the dissertation of von Scherer, the book of Beaupré and the report of Krantz, and numerous monographs, has brought to light valuable papers of soldiers who had returned and had left their remembrances of life of the soldiers during the Russian campaign to their descendants and relatives who had kept these papers a sacred inheritance during one hundred years.

The picture in the foreground of all histories of the Russian campaign is the shadow of the great warrior who led the troops, in whose invincibility all men who followed him in 1812 believed and by whom they stood in their soldier's honour, with a constancy without equal, a steadfastness which merits our admiration.

Three fourths of the whole army belonged to nations whose real interests were in direct opposition to the war against Russia. Notwithstanding that many were aware of this fact, they fought as brave in battle as if their own highest interests were at stake. All wanted to uphold their own honour as men and the honour of their nations. And no matter how the individual soldier was thinking of Napoleon, whether he loved or hated him, there was not a single one in the whole army who did not have implicit confidence in his talent. Wherever the Emperor showed himself the soldiers believed in victory, where he appeared thousands of men shouted from the depth of their heart and with all the power of their voices *Vive l'Empereur!*

A wild martial spirit reigned in all lands, the bloody sword did not ask why and against whom it was drawn. To win glory for the own army, the own colours and standards was the parole of the day. All the masses of different nations felt as belonging to one great whole and were determined to act as such.

And all this has to be considered in a medical history of the campaign of 1812.

Throughout Germany, Napoleon is the favourite hero. In the homes of the common people, in the huts of the peasants, there are pictures ornamenting the walls, engravings which have turned yellow from age, the frames of which are worm eaten. These pictures represent a variety of subjects, but rarely are there pictures missing of scenes of the life of Napoleon. Generally they are divided into fields, and in the larger middle field you see the hero of small stature, on a white horse, from his sallow face the cold calculating eyes looking into a throng of bayonets, lances, bearskin caps, helmets, and proud eagles.

The graceful mouth, in contrast to the strong projecting chin, modifies somewhat the severity of this face, a face of marble of which it has been said that it gave the impression of a field of death, and the man with this face is accustomed to conquer, to reign, to destroy. He is the inexorable God of war himself, not in glittering armour, but in a plain uniform ornamented with one single order for personal bravery. The tuft of hair on his high and broad forehead is like a sign of everlasting scorn. A gloomy, dreadfully attractive figure. In some of the pictures we see him in his plain gray overcoat and well-known hat, surrounded by marshals in splendid dress parade, forming a contrast to the simplicity of their master, on some elevation from which he looks into burning cities; again we see him unmoved by dreadful surroundings, riding through battle scenes of horror.

Over my desk hangs such an old steel engraving, given to me by an old German lady who told me that her father had thought a great deal of it. On Saturdays he would wash the glass over the other pictures with water, but for washing the Napoleon picture he would use alcohol.

Before this man kings have trembled, innumerable thousands have cheerfully given their blood, their lives; this man has been adored like a God and cursed like a devil. He has been the fate of the world until his hour struck. Many say providence had selected him to castigate the universe and its enslaved peoples. A great German historian, Gervinus, has said: "He was the greatest benefactor of Germany who removed the gloriole from the heads crowned by the grace of God." He accomplished great things because he had great power, he committed great faults because he was so powerful. Without his unrestricted power he could not have accomplished one nor committed the other.

History is logic. Whenever great wrongs prevail, some mighty men appear and arouse the people, and these extraordinary men are like the storm in winter which shatters and breaks what is rotten, preparing for spring.

The German schoolboy, when he learns of the greatest warriors and conquerors, of Alexander the Great, of Julius Caesar, is most fascinated when he hears the history of the greatest of all the warriors of the world, the history of Napoleon, and he is spellbound reading the awfully beautiful histories concerning his unheard of deeds, his rise without example, and his sudden downfall.

And he, the great man, the soldier-emperor, he rides on his white horse in the boy's dreams, just as depicted on the engravings upon which the boys look with a kind of holy awe.

The son of a Corsican lawyer, becoming in early manhood the master of the world, what could inflame youthful fiction more than this wonderful career?

All great conquerors come to a barrier. Alexander, when he planned to subdue India, found the barrier at the Indus. Caesar found it at the Thames and at the Rhine. Our hero's fate was to be fulfilled at Moscow. His insatiable thirst to rule had led him into Russia. He stood at the height of his power and glory. Holland, Italy, a part of Germany, were French, and Germany especially groaned under the heel of severe xenocraty. The old German Empire had broken down, nothing of it was left but a ridiculous name, "*Römisches Reich deutscher Nation*." The crowned heads of Germany held their thrones merely by the grace of Napoleon. Only Spain, united with England, dared him yet. Since Napoleon could not attack the English directly, on account of their power at sea, he tried to hit them where they were most sensitive, at their pocket. He instituted the continental *blocus*. Russia with the other lands of Continental Europe had to close her ports and markets against England, but Russia soon became tired of this pressure and preferred a new war with Napoleon to French domination.

In giving this sketch of the popularity of Napoleon's memory in Germany, I have availed myself of a German calendar for the year 1913, called *Der Lahrer hinkende Bote*.

Except the English translation of Beaupré's book I have taken from French and German writings only.

I desire to thank Mr. S. Simonis, of New York, who has revised the entire manuscript and read the proofs; next to him I am under obligations to Reichs Archiv Rat Dr. Striedinger, of Munich, and Mr. Franz Herrmann, of New York, who have loaned me most valuable books and pointed out important literature, and finally to Miss F. de Cerkez, who has aided me in the translation of some of the chapters.

Crossing the Niemen

On May 10th, 1812, the *Moniteur* published the following note:

The emperor has left today to inspect the Grand Army united at the Vistula.

In France, in all parts of the Empire, the lassitude was extreme and the misery increasing, there was no commerce, with dearth pronounced in twenty provinces, sedition of the hungry had broken out in Normandy, the *gendarmes* pursuing the "refractories" everywhere, and blood was shed in all thirty departments.

There was the complaint of exhausted population, and loudest was the complaint of mothers whose sons had been killed in the war.

Napoleon was aware of these evils and understood well their gravity, but he counted on his usual remedy, new victories; saying to himself that a great blow dealt in the north, throwing Russia and indirectly England at his feet, would again be the salvation of the situation.

Caulaincourt, his ambassador to the *Tzar*, had told him in several conversations, one of which had lasted seven hours, that he would find more terrible disaster in Russia than in Spain, that his army would be destroyed in the vastness of the country by the iron climate, that the *Tzar* would retire to the farthest Asiatic provinces rather than accept a dishonourable peace, that the Russians would retreat but never cede.

Napoleon listened attentively to these prophetic words, showing surprise and emotion; then he fell into a profound reflection, but at the end of his revery, having enumerated once more his armies, all his people, he said: "Bah! a good battle will bring to reason the good determination of your friend Alexander."

And in his entourage there were many who shared his optimism. The brilliant youth of that new aristocracy which had begun to fill his staff was anxious to equal the old soldiers of the revolution, the plebeian heroes.

They prepared for war in a luxurious way and ordered sumptuous outfits and equipages which later on encumbered the roads of Germany, just as the carriages of the Prussian army had done in 1806. These French officers spoke of the Russian campaign as a six months' hunting party.

Napoleon had calculated not to occupy the country between the Vistula and the Niemen before the end of May, when the late spring of those regions would have covered the fields with green, so that the 100 thousand horses marching with the army could find feed.

He traversed Germany between a double lane of kings, and princes bowed in an attitude of adoration.

He found them at Mainz, at Wuerzburg, at Bamberg, and his advance might be compared to the royal progress of an Asiatic potentate.

Whole populations were turned out to salute him, and during the night the route over which the imperial carriages passed was illuminated by lighted piles of wood—an extensive line of fire in his honour.

At Dresden he had the attendance of an emperor (that of Austria) and of kings and reigning princes, who were present at his levees, together with their prime ministers (the better to catch, to report, the words he said, however insignificant) while high German dignitaries waited on him at the table.

The Emperor and the Empress of Austria had come at their own desire to salute their daughter and their son-in-law and to present their good wishes for the success of the great expedition.

Twelve days in succession he had at dinner the Emperor and Empress of Austria, the King and Queen of Saxony, the Saxon princes, the Prince Primate of the Confederation of the Rhine—even the King of Prussia was present; he offered his son for adjutant, which offer, however, Napoleon was tactful enough not to accept.

All the kings and reigning princes from the other States of Germany presented their best wishes and pledged faithfulness to Napoleon in his war against Russia.

Around the French emperor and empress at Dresden there was a court the like of which Europe had never seen and never will see again.

A *Te Deum* was sung to thank heaven for his arrival; there was a magnificent display of fireworks, but the climax of all was a great concert with an apotheosis showing, as the principal figure, the sun with the inscription: "Less great and less beautiful than He." "It appears that these people take me for very stupid," said Napoleon to this, shrugging his shoulders.

In speaking to one of his intimates he called the King of Prussia a sergeant instructor, *une bête*, but openly he treated him with great courtesy.

He made rich presents: gold and enamelled boxes, jewellery and portraits of himself enriched with costly stones. During the happy days of Dresden he enjoyed for once an intimate family life.

On one occasion he held a long conversation with his father-in-law, during which he developed his plans of the Russian campaign, with minute and endless military details of which the emperor of Austria, being no strategist at all, understood nothing and said afterward: "My son-in-law is alright here," pointing to the heart, "but here"— pointing to the forehead—he made a significant gesture.

This criticism of Napoleon by the Emperor of Austria became popular and has been accepted by many writers. All reproaches about Cesarian insanity which were cast at the great man and his whole life date from that time. Some have said that he wanted to conquer England and Russia because these two he considered the arch enemies of Europe, that he foresaw the threatening growth of these two countries as dangerous, and if he did not take advantage of the good opportunity the future of Europe would be at the mercy of Russia and England.

The conquest of Russia was the keynote of his universal policy.

The much calumniated *blocus*, say other writers, would finally have been the greatest blessing for continental Europe; its aim had already been attained in so far as many London houses failed, and famine reigned on the British islands in consequence of the high cost of living.

And these writers say Napoleon had by no means become insane, but, on the contrary, frightfully clear. Another explanation given was that he worried about his dynasty, his child, entertaining fear that his empire might fall to pieces after his death, like the empire of Charles the Great.

Although he was enjoying good health, he had been warned by his physician, Corvisart, of cancer of the stomach, from which Napoleon's father had died. Some suspicious black specks had been observed in the vomit. Therefore no time was to be lost, all had to be done in haste.

The rupture originated with Russia, for at the end of the year 1810 the *Tzar* annulled the *blocus* and even excluded French goods or placed an inordinate duty on them—this was, in fact, a declaration of war. Russia wanted war while the Spanish campaign was taxing France's military forces.

The only reliable report of Napoleon's communications at St. Helena has been given by General de Gourgaud in the diary which he kept while with the emperor from 1815 to 1818, and which has been published in the year 1898. Here is what Napoleon said on this subject:

On June 13th, 1816, he remarked in conversation with Gourgaud:

> I did not want the war with Russia, but Kurakin presented me a threatening note on account of Davout's troops at Hamburg. Bassano and Champagny were mediocre ministers, they did not comprehend the intention which had dictated that note. I myself could not argue with Kurakin. They persuaded me that it meant declaration of war. Russia had taken off several divisions from Moldavia and would take the initiative with an attack on Warsaw. Kurakin threatened and asked for his passports. I myself believed finally they wanted war. I mobilized! I sent Lauriston to Alexander, but he was not even received. From Dresden I sent Narbonne, everything convinced me that Russia wanted war. I crossed the Niemen near Wilna.
>
> Alexander sent a General to me to assure me that he did not wish war; I treated this ambassador very well, he dined with me, but I believed his mission was a trick to prevent the cutting off of Bagratian. I therefore continued the march.
>
> I did not wish to declare war against Russia, but I had the impression that Russia wanted to break with me. I knew very well the difficulties of such a campaign.

Gourgaud wrote in his diary a conversation which he had with Montholon on July 9th, 1817:

> What was the real motive of the Russian campaign? I know nothing about it, and perhaps the Emperor himself did not know it. Did he intend to go to India after having dethroned the Moscowitic dynasty? The preparations, the tents which he took along, seem to suggest this assumption.

Montholon answered:

> According to the instructions which I, as ambassador, received I believe that His Majesty wanted to become Emperor of Germany, that he aimed to be crowned as '*Emperor of the West*'. The Rhenish Confederation was made to understand this idea. In Erfurt it was already a foregone conclusion, but Alexander demanded Constantinople, and this Napoleon would not concede.

At another conversation Napoleon admitted:

> I have been too hasty. I should have remained a whole year at the Niemen and in Prussia, in order to give my troops the much needed rest, to reorganize the army and also to eat up Prussia.

All these details, Napoleon's admission included, show that nobody knew and nobody knows why this gigantic expedition was undertaken. Certain is, however, that England had a hand in the break between Napoleon and Alexander.

When Napoleon called on the generals to lead them into this expedition they all had become settled to some extent, some in Paris, others on their possessions or as governors and commanders all over Europe, which at that time meant France; in consequence there existed a certain displeasure among these officers, especially among the older ones and those of high rank.

The high positions which he had created for them and the rich incomes which they enjoyed had developed their and their wives' taste for a luxurious and brilliant mode of living. Besides, most of them, as well as their master, had attained the age between forty and fifty, their ambition gradually had relented, they had enough; and the family with which they had been together for very brief periods only between two campaigns, clung to them now and held them tightly.

Notwithstanding these conditions, they all came when the Emperor called; after they had shaken off wife and children and had mounted in the saddle, while the old veterans and the young impatient soldiers were jubilant around them, they regained their good humour and went on to new victories, the brave men they always had been.

Especially at first when, at the head of their magnificent regiments, they marched eastward through the conquered lands, from city to city, from castle to castle, like masters of the world, when in Dresden they met their comrades in war and their friends, and when they saw how all the crowned heads of Europe bowed before their Emperor, then the Grand Army was in its glory.

As we know from history the Grand Army had contingents from twenty nationalities: Frenchmen, Germans, Italians, Austrians, Swiss, Spaniards, Portuguese, Poles, Illyrians, etc., and numbered over half a million men, with 100 thousand horses, 1,000 cannon.

According to Bleibtreu (*Die grosse Armee*, Stuttgart, 1908), and Kielland (*Rings um Napoleon*, Leipzig, 1907) the Grand Army was made up as follows:

First Corps—Davout, six divisions of the best troops under the command of Morand, Friant, Gudin. In this corps were, besides French, Badensian, Dutch, and Polish regiments. Davout commanded also 17 thousand Prussian soldiers under General Grawert. Among the generals were Compans and Pajol, the engineer Haxo, and the handsome General Friederich   67,000
Second Corps—Oudinot with the divisions of Generals Merle, Legrand, Maison, Lannes' and Massena's veterans   40,000
Third Corps—Ney with two divisions of veterans of Lannes; to this corps belonged the Wuerttembergians who had served under Ney before   49,000
Fourth Corps—Prince Eugene with Junot as second commander, and the Generals Grouchy, Broussier, the two brothers Delzon. In this corps were the best soldiers of the Italian army   45,000
Fifth Corps—Prince Poniatowski. Soldiers of all arms, mostly Poles 26,000 Sixth Corps—General St Cyr. Mostly foreigners who had served in the French army since 1809   25,000
The Sixth Corps—General St Cyr. Mostly foreigners who had served in the French army since 1809   25,000
The Seventh Corps—General Reynier. Mostly Saxons and Poles   17,000
The Eighth Corps—King Jerome. Westphalians and Hessians
                     18,000

Besides, there were four corps of reserve cavalry distributed among the corps of Davout, Oudinot, and Ney; the rest, excellent horsemen, marched with the Imperial Guard   15,000
The Imperial Guards were commanded by the Marshals Mortier and Lefebvre and were divided into two corps, the old guard and the young guard   47,000

16

There was the engineer park, composed of sappers, miners, pontooneers and military mechanicians of all descriptions, the artillery park, and train of wagons with attendants and horses. To these two trains alone belonged 18 thousand horses.

In the active army which marched toward Russia there were 423 thousand well drilled soldiers; namely, 300 thousand infantry, seventy thousand cavalry and thirty thousand artillery with one thousand cannon, six pontoon trains, ambulances, and also provisions for one month.

As reserve, the ninth corps—Marshal Victor—and the tenth corps—Augereau—were stationed near Magdeburg, ready to complete the army gradually.

The whole army which marched to Russia consisted of 620 thousand men.

The question of subsistence for this immense body occupied Napoleon chiefly. He felt the extraordinary difficulty and great danger, he knew that at the moment of coming in contact with the enemy all the corps would be out of supplies in twenty or twenty-five days if there were no great reserves of bread, biscuit, rice, etc., closely following the army.

His system was that of requisition. To secure the needed supplies the commanders of the corps were ordered to seize in the country all the grain which could be found and at once to convert it into flour, with methodic activity.

Napoleon himself superintended and hastened the work. At twenty different places along the Vistula he had the grinding done unceasingly, distributing the flour thus obtained among the corps and expediting its transport by every possible means. He even invented new measures for this purpose, among which the well-known formation of battalions of cattle, an immense rolling stock destined to follow the columns to serve twofold: for transportation of provisions, and finally as food.

With the beginning of June these supreme preparations had been made or seemed to have been made. In the lands through which the troops were to march before they reached the Niemen, the spring had done its work; there was abundance of forage.

Napoleon had impatiently awaited this time during ten months of secret activity.

It was the hope of Russia and the fear of those Frenchmen who understood the Russian climate that the campaign would drag into the winter.

Russians already told of the village blacksmith who laughed when he was shown a French horseshoe which had been found on the road, and said: "Not one of these horses will leave Russia if the army remains till frost sets in!" The French horseshoes had neither pins nor barbed hooks, and it would be impossible for horses thus shod to draw cannons and heavy wagons up and down hill over frozen and slippery roads.

The annihilation of the Grand Army is not to be attributed to the cold and the fearful conditions on the retreat from Moscow alone, the army was in reality annihilated before it reached Russia, as we shall see by the following description which I have taken from a Latin dissertation (translated also into German) of the surgeon of a Wuerttembergian regiment, Ch. Io. von Scherer, who had served through the whole campaign and in the year 1820 had submitted this dissertation, "*Historia Morborum, qui in Expeditione Contra Russiam Anno 1812 Facta Legiones Wuerttembergicas invaserunt, praesertim eorum qui frigore orti sunt,*" to the Medical Faculty, presided over by F. G. Gmelin, to obtain the degree of doctor of medicine.

The diseases which befell the soldiers in Russia extended over the whole army. Von Scherer, however, gives his own observations only, which he had made while serving in the Wuerttembergian corps of fourteen to fifteen thousand men.

The expedition into Russia in the year 1812 was divided into ten divisions, each of these numbering fifty to sixty thousand men, all healthy, robust, most of them hardened in war. The Wuerttembergians were commanded by General Count von Scheeler and the French General Marchand; the highest commander was Marshal Ney.

In the beginning of May, 1812, the great army of Napoleon arrived at the frontier of Poland, whence it proceeded by forced and most tiresome marches to the river Niemen, which forms the boundary between Lithuania and Poland, arriving at the borders of the river in the middle of June.

An immense body of soldiers (500,000) met near the city of Kowno, crossed the Niemen on pontoons, and formed, under the eyes of the emperor, in endless battle line on the other side.

The forced march continued day and night over the sandy soil of Poland. The tropical heat during the day and the low temperature at night, the frequent rainstorms from the north, the camping on bare and often wet ground, the ever increasing want of pure water and fresh provisions, the immense masses of dust, which, cloudlike, hung over the marching columns—all these difficulties put together had sapped the strength of the soldiers already at the beginning of the campaign. Many were taken sick before they reached the Niemen.

The march through Lithuania was hastened as much as the march through Poland. Provisions became scarcer all the time, meat from cattle that had suffered from starvation and exhaustion was for a long time the soldiers' only food. The great heat, and the inhalation of sand and dust, dried the tissues of the body, and the thirsty soldiers longed in vain for a drink of water. Often there was no other opportunity to quench the thirst than the water afforded by the swamps. The officers were powerless to prevent the soldiers from kneeling down at stagnant pools and drinking the foul water without stint.

Thus the army, tired to the utmost from overexertion and privation, and disposed to sickness, entered the land of the enemy. The forced marches were continued during the day, through sand and dust, until stormy weather set in with rain, followed by cold winds.

With the appearance of bad weather, dysentery, which had already been observed at the time of the crossing of the Niemen, showed itself with greater severity. The route the army had taken from camp to camp was marked by offensive evacuations. The number of the sick became so great that they could not all be attended to, and medical treatment became illusory when the supply of medicaments was exhausted.

The greater part of the army fought in vain, however courageously, against the extending evil. As everything was wanting of which the sick were in need, there was no barrier against the spread of the disease, while at the same time the privations and hardships which had caused it continued and reached their climax.

Some of these soldiers would march, equipped with knapsack and arms, apparently in good spirits, but suddenly would succumb and die. Others, especially those of strong constitution, would become melancholy and commit suicide. The number of deaths increased from day to day.

Marvellous was the effect of emotion on the disease. Surgeon-General von Kohlreuter, during and after the battle of Smolensk, witnessed this influence. Of four thousand Wuerttembergians who took part in that battle, there were few quite free from dysentery.

Tired and depressed, the army dragged along; but as soon as the soldiers heard the cannon in the distance, telling them the battle was beginning, they emerged at once from their lethargy; the expression of their faces, which had been one of sadness, changed to one of joy and hilarity. Joyfully and with great bravery they went into action. During the four days that the battle lasted, and for some days afterward, dysentery disappeared as if banished by magic. When the battle was over and the privations were the same again as they had been, the disease returned with the same severity as before—nay, even worse, and the soldiers fell into complete lethargy.

The necropsy of those who had died from dysentery revealed derangement of the digestive organs; the stomach, the large intestine, mostly the rectum, were inflamed; the *intima* of stomach and duodenum, sometime the whole intestine, were atonic. In some cases there were small ulcers, with jagged margins, in the stomach, especially in its *fundus*, and in the rectum; in other cases dysentery had proceeded to such an extent that pretty large ulcers had developed, extending from the stomach into the small and from there into the large intestine, into the rectum. These ulcers were of sizes varying from that of a lentil to the size of a walnut.

Where the disease had been progressive the *intima*, the mucosa and *submucosa*—very seldom, however, the *serosa*—were perforated by ulcers; in many cases there were gangrenous patches in the *fundus* of the stomach and along the intestinal tract. The gastric juice smelled highly acid, frequently the liver was discoloured and contained a bluish liquid, its lower part in most cases hardened and bluish; the gall bladder, as a rule, was empty or contained only a small amount of bile; the mesenteric glands were mostly inflamed, sometimes purulent; the mesenteric and visceral vessels appeared often as if studded with blood. Such patients had suffered sometimes from gastralgy, had had a great craving for food, especially vegetables, but were during that time entirely free from fever.

Remarkably sudden disaster followed the immoderate use of alcohol. Some Wuerttembergian soldiers, who during the first days of July had been sent on requisition, had discovered large quantities of brandy in a nobleman's mansion, and had indulged in its immoderate use and died, like all dysentery patients who took too much alcohol.

The number of Wuerttembergians afflicted with dysentery, while on the march from the Niemen to the Dwina, amounted to three thousand, at least this many were left behind in the hospitals of Malaty, Wilna, Disna, Strizzowan and Witepsk. The number of deaths in the hospitals increased as the disease proceeded, from day to day, and the number of those who died on the march was not small. Exact hospital statistics cannot be given except of Strizzowan, which was the only hospital from which lists had been preserved; and here von Scherer did duty during six weeks. Out of 902 patients 301 died during the first three weeks; during the other three weeks when the patients had better care only thirty-six died.

In the hospitals established on the march, in haste, in poor villages, medicaments were either wanting entirely or could be had only in insufficient quantity. All medical plants which grew on the soil in that climate were utilized by the surgeons, as, for instance in the hospital of Witepsk, huckleberries and the root of tormentilla. Establishing the hospital in Strizzowan von Scherer placed some of his patients in the castle, others in a barn and the rest in stables. Not without great difficulties and under dangers he procured provisions from the neighbourhood. As medicaments he used, and sometimes with really good results, the following plants which were found in abundance in the vicinity: 1. *Cochlearia armoracia*; 2. *Acorus calamus*; 3. *Allium sativum*; 4. *Raphanus sativus;* 5. *Menyanthes trifoliata*; 6. *Salvia officinalis*.

In the course of the following three weeks General Count von Scheeler handed him several thousand florins to be used for the alleviation of the sufferings of the soldiers under his care, and von Scherer procured from great distances, namely, from the Polish cities Mohilew, Minsk and Wilna, suitable medicines and provisions. The proper diet which could now be secured, together with best medicines, had an excellent effect. This is seen at a glance when perusing the statistics of the first three and the last three weeks. In some cases in which the patients had been on the way to recovery, insignificant causes would bring relapse. Potatoes grew in abundance in the vicinity of the hospital, and patients would clandestinely help themselves and eat them in excessive quantities, with fatal result.

In some the intestinal tract remained very weak for a long time. Emaciation of the convalescents improved only very slowly. Remarkable was a certain mental depression or indolence which remained in many patients. Even in officers who von Scherer had known as energetic and good-humoured men there was seen for a long time a morose condition and very noticeable dulness. Whatever they undertook was done slowly and imperfectly. Sometimes, even with a kind of wickedness, they showed an inclination to steal or do something forbidden. Sometimes it was difficult to induce them to take exercise. Von Scherer, in order to cheer up the convalescents, ordered daily walks under guard, and this was the more necessary as *oedemata* developed on the extremities in those who remained motionless on their couches.

How injurious the immoderate use of alcoholic beverages proved to be was demonstrated in three cases of convalescents, who were still somewhat weak. They had secretly procured some bottles of brandy from the cellar of the hospital, and with the idea of having a good time had drunk all of it in one sitting. Very soon they had dangerous symptoms: abdominal pain, nausea and vomiting followed by lachrymation from the protruding and inflamed eyes. They fell down senseless, had liquid and highly offensive evacuations and died, in spite of all medical aid, in six hours. On the abdomen, the neck, the chest and especially on the feet of the corpses of these men there were gangrenous spots of different sizes, a plain proof that the acute inflammation, gangrene and putrefaction had been caused by the excessive irritation of the extremely weak body. Circumstances forbade necropsy in these cases.

Among different publications on the medical history of Napoleon's campaign in 1812, which I happened to find, was a dissertation of Marin Bunoust, *Considerations générales sur la congelation pendant l'ivresse observée en Russie en 1812*. Paris, 1817 (published, therefore, three years before publication of von Scherer's dissertation), in which the author wishes to show that the physiological effect of drunkenness on the organism is identical with that of extreme cold.

Von Scherer, after the hospital of Strizzowan had been evacuated, again joined his regiment. The French army in forced marches pursued the enemy on the road to Moscow over Ostrowno, Witepsk and Smolensk. Dysentery did not abate. In the hospitals of Smolensk, Wiasma and Ghiat, von Scherer found, besides the wounded from the Battles of Krasnoe, Smolensk and Borodino, a great number of dysentery patients; many died on the march. The whole presented a pitiful sight, and the soldiers' contempt of life excited horror.

We shall return to von Scherer's dissertation when describing the retreat from Moscow.

While the dissertation of von Scherer treats on the fate of the Wuerttembergian corps of Napoleon's grand army, a memoir of First Lieutenant von Borcke who served as adjutant of General von Ochs in the Westphalian corps relates the fate of the Westphalians in the grand army of 1812.

The Westphalians, 23,747 men strong, left Cassel in the month of March, 1812, to unite with the French army. One of the regiments was sent later and joined the corps while the army was on the retreat from Moscow at Moshaisk. This regiment, like another, which followed still later and joined the army on the retreat at Wilna, was annihilated. Of the 23,747 men a few hundred finally returned. On March 24th, the Westphalians crossed the Elbe, von Borcke (it is a common error in American literature to spell the predicate of nobility *von* with a capital V when at the beginning of a period, while neither *von* nor the corresponding French *de* as predicate of nobility should ever be spelled with a capital) at that time suffered from intermittent fever, but was cured by the use of calisaya bark. I mention this to call attention to the fact that quinine was not known in the year 1812. When the corps marched into Poland the abundance of provisions which the soldiers had enjoyed, came to an end.

There were no magazines from which rations could have been distributed, and the poor Polish peasants, upon whom requisitions should have been made, had nothing for the soldiers. Disorder among the troops who thus far distinguished themselves by strictest discipline, made its appearance. How the army was harassed by the plague of dysentery, how the soldiers were marching during great heat, insufficiently supplied in every way, and how they suffered from manifold hardships, has been described in von Scherer's dissertation. The Westphalian corps was in as precarious a condition as the Wuerttembergian, as in fact the whole army and the Westphalian battalions were already reduced to one-half their former number. Many soldiers had remained behind on account of sickness or exhaustion, and officers were sent back to bring them to the ranks again.

The whole army would have dissolved if the march had not been interrupted. Napoleon ordered a stay. An order from him called for a rally of the troops, for the completion of war material, ammunition, and horses and provisions; but where to take all these things from? The war had not yet begun, and the troops were already in danger of starvation. Only with sadness and fear could the soldiers, under these circumstances, look into the future.

In what way, says Ebstein, can this great want, this insufficient supply of provisions, which made itself felt even at the beginning of the campaign, be explained? It has been shown how Napoleon exerted himself to meet the extraordinary difficulty of supplying the grand army of half a million of men and 100,000 horses with provisions, how well he was aware of the great danger in this regard, how he superintended and hastened the work of providing for men and horses by every possible means, that he understood all the circumstances surrounding the march of the grand army through a vast country populated by few, and these mostly serfs who had barely sufficient food for themselves and no means to replenish their stock in case it should have been exhausted by Napoleon's system of requisition, not to speak of the marauding to which the French soldiers were soon forced to resort.

Ebstein says that the cause of the sad, the wretched condition concerning supplies was due to the fact that incompetent officers had been appointed as commissaries of the army; they held high military rank, were independent and could not be easily reached for their faults. It happened that soldiers were starving near well filled magazines, such magazines at Kowno, Wilna, Minsk, Orcha being not only well, but over, filled, while the passing troops were in dire need. We shall later on come to frightful details of this kind.

The miserable maintenance had from the beginning a demoralizing effect on the men, manifested by desertion, insubordination, marauding, vandalism. General Sir Robert Wilson, British commissioner with the headquarters of the Russian Army, quoted by Ebstein, says:

> The French Army, from its very entrance into the Russian territory (and this cannot be repeated too often to lend the proper weight to the consequences resulting therefrom), notwithstanding order on order and some exemplary punishments, had been incorrigibly guilty of every excess. It had not only seized with violence all that its wants demanded, but destroyed in mere wantonness what did not tempt its cupidity. No vandal ferocity was ever more destructive. Those crimes, however, were not committed with impunity. Want, sickness, and an enraged peasantry, inflicted terrible reprisals, and caused daily a fearful reduction of numbers.

But this description of the Englishman will apply to every army in which there are such difficulties in obtaining the necessary supplies as they existed here on the forced marches.

Further, he does not speak of the severe punishments meted out to the culprits. By order of Napoleon entire squads of marauders were shot. Von Roos, chief physician of a Wuerttembergian regiment, has seen that before their execution they had to dig their own graves.

In Wilna already Davout ordered the execution of seventy, and in Minsk of thirteen marauders.

A Westphalian officer, von Lossberg, commander of a battalion, wrote in his letters to his wife—which are of great value to the history of the campaign—from Toloschin on July 25:

> On our march we met a detachment of Davout's corps; they shot before our eyes a commissary of the army who had been condemned to death for fraud. He had sold for 200 dollars provisions which had been intended for the soldiers.

Napoleon had stayed several days at Thorn, inspecting the departing troops, visiting the magazines, bestowing a last glance upon everything. Before the guards left their cantonments he wanted to see the different corps and hold a great review. He loved to see again the manly figures of the soldiers, their chests of iron, these braves who stood before him, immovable in parade, irresistible in fight. Their bearing and their expression gave him pleasure. Notwithstanding the fatigues and the privations of the march, enthusiasm shone on all the faces, in the brightening of all the eyes. He wanted to give with his own mouth the order "forward march" to the regiments of the guard, and he saw the endless defile of these proud uniforms, heard the uninterrupted beating of the drums, the sound of the trumpets, the acclamation "*Vive l'Empereur*" of the beautiful troops, the departure of the officers, every one of whom had orders to set in motion or to halt human masses.

All this great movement around him, by his will, at his word, animated and excited him. Now, the lot having irrevocably been cast, he surrenders himself completely to his instincts as warrior, he feels himself only soldier, the greatest and most ardent who has existed, he dreams of nothing but victories and conquests. At night, after having given orders all day long, he slept only at intervals, passing part of the night walking up and down. One night those on duty, who slept near his room, were surprised hearing him sing with plain voice a popular song of the soldiers of the republic.

On June 6th, Napoleon left Thorn while all the army was marching. At Danzig he saw Murat, whom he had called directly from Naples. He did not wish him near except for the fight where he would be an ornament in battle and set a magnificent example. Otherwise he considered his presence useless and hurtful. He had taken special pains to keep him away from Dresden, from the assembly of sovereigns, from contact with dynasties of the *ancien régime*, especially of the house of Austria, because of his being a king of recent origin. He feared the indiscretion of the newly made kings when brought together with the sovereigns by the grace of God. He did not wish that any intimacy should develop between them.

The meeting of the two brothers-in-law was at first cold and painful. Each had a grievance against the other and did not restrain himself at all to pronounce it. Murat complained, as he had done before, that he, as King of Naples, was an instrument of domination and tyranny, and added that he could find a way to extricate himself from such an intolerable exigency. Napoleon reproached Murat of his more and more marked inclination to disobey, of his digression in language and conduct, and of his suspicious actions. He looked at him with a severe mien, spoke harsh words, and treated him altogether with severity. But then, suddenly changing his tone, he spoke to him in a language of friendship, of wounded and misunderstood friendship, became emotional, complained of ingratitude, and recalled the memory of their long affection, their military comradery. The king who was easily moved, was thinking of all the generosity he had enjoyed, and could not resist the appeal, he became emotional in his turn, almost shed tears, forgot all grief for a while, and was conquered.

And in the evening before his intimates the emperor lauded himself for having played excellent comedy to regain Murat, that he had by turns and very successfully enacted anger and sentimentality with this Italian *pantaleone*, but, added he, Murat has a good heart.

Ahead of the emperor, between Danzig and Koenigsberg, traversing East Prussia and some districts of Poland, marched the army—under what difficulties has been described. At the same time, through the Baltic and the Frische Haff, came the more ponderous war material, the pontoons and the heaviest artillery, the siege guns. To complete the supply of provisions before entering upon the campaign the troops exhausted the land by making extensive requisitions. The emperor had wished that all should go on regularly and that everything taken from the inhabitants should be paid for, but this the soldiers did not consider. They took and emptied the granaries, tore down the straw from the roofs of the peasants' houses, barns, and stables to make litter for their horses, and treated the inhabitants not as friends, but as if they were people of a conquered land.

The cavalry which passed first helped themselves for their horses to all the hay and all the grass, the artillery and the train were obliged to take from the fields the green barley and oats, and the army altogether ruined the population where it passed. The men obliged to disperse during a part of the day as foragers, got into the habit of disbanding and of looseness of discipline, and the impossibility manifested itself to keep in order and in ranks the multitude of different races, different in languages, who with their many vehicles represented a regular migration.

Everything became monotonous—the country, the absence of an enemy. They found Prussia and especially Poland, ugly, dirty, miserable, all the houses were full of dirt and vermin, domestic animals of all kinds were the intimate *syntrophoi* of the peasants in their living rooms. The soldiers bore badly the inconvenience of the lodging, the coolness of the night following the burning heat of the day, the fogs in the mornings. But they consoled themselves with illusions, painting the future in rosy colours, hoping to find across the Niemen a better soil, a different people, more favourable to the soldier, and longed for Russia as for the promised land.

The Grand Army had arrived at the Niemen. It was on June 24th, the sun rose radiant and lightened with his fire a magnificent scene. To the troops was read a short and energetic proclamation. Napoleon came out of his tent, surrounded by his officers, and contemplated with his field glass the sight of this prodigious force; hundreds of thousands of soldiers united in one place! One could not find anything comparable to the enthusiasm which the presence of Napoleon inspired on that day. The right bank of the river was covered with these magnificent troops; they descended from the heights and spread out in long files over the three bridges, resembling three currents; the rays of the sun glittered on the bayonets and helmets, and the cry *Vive l'Empereur!* was heard incessantly.

If I were to give a full description to do justice to the magnificent spectacle I would have to quote from the journals of that epoch, and if I were a painter I could not find a greater subject for my art.

On to Moscow

Arrived in Russia the French were soon disappointed; gloomy forests and sterile soil met the eye, all was sad and silent. After the army had passed the Niemen and entered into Poland the misery, instead of diminishing, increased, the hour had struck for these unfortunates. The enemy destroyed everything on retreating, the cattle were taken to distant provinces; the French saw the destruction of the fields, the villages were deserted, the peasants fled upon the appearance of the French army, all inhabitants had left except the Jews. When the army came to Lithuania everything seemed to be in league against the French. It was a rainy season, the soldiers marched through vast and gloomy forests, and all was melancholy.

One could have imagined himself to be in a desert if it had not been for the vehicles, the cursing of the drivers, discontented on account of hunger and fatigue, the imprecations of the soldiers on every occasion; bad humour, due to privations, prevailed everywhere. It would seem as if the furies of hell were marching at the heels of the army. The roads were in a terrible condition, almost unpassable on account of the rain which had been continuous since the crossing of the Niemen; the artillery wagons especially gave great trouble in passing marshes, and, on account of the extreme exhaustion of the horses, a great many of these vehicles had to be abandoned. The horses receiving no nourishment but green herbs could resist even less than the men and they fell by the hundred.

The improper feeding of the animals caused gastric disturbances, alternately diarrhoea and constipation, enormous tympanitis, peritonitis. It is touching to read of the devotion of German cavalrymen to their poor horses. They would introduce the whole arm into the bowel to relieve the suffering creatures of the accumulated fecal masses.

As the army advanced over these roads the extreme want of provisions was bitterly felt. The warriors already reduced to such an excess of misery were exposed to rain without being able to dry themselves; to nourish themselves they were forced to resort to the most horrible marauding, and sometimes they had nothing to eat for twenty-four hours or even longer. They ran through the land in all directions, disregarding all dangers, sometimes many miles away from the route, to find provisions.

Wherever they came they went through the houses from the foundation to the roof, and when they found animals they took them away; no attention was paid to the feeling of the poor peasants and nothing was considered as being too harsh for them; in most instances the latter had run away for fear of maltreatment. Nothing is so afflicting as to see the rapacity of pillaging soldiers, stealing and destroying everything coming under their hands. They took to excess vodka found in the magazines which the enemy had not destroyed, or in the castles off the main route. In consequence of this abuse of alcohol while in their feeble condition many perished. The enemy retreated behind the Dwina and fortified himself in camp. It was thought that he would give battle, and all enjoyed this prospect.

On July 20, at a time when the conditions of the army were already terrible, the heat became excessive. The rains ceased; there were no rainy days, except an occasional storm, until September 17. The poor infantrymen were to be pitied; they had to carry their arms, their effects, their cartridges, harassed by continuous fatigue, overpowered by hunger and a thousand sorrows, and were obliged to march 10, 12, 15, and sometimes even 16 and 17 miles a day over dusty roads under a burning sun, all the time tormented by a cruel thirst. But all this has been fully described in an earlier chapter.

On July 23 the Prince of Eckmühl (Davout) had a very hot engagement with the Russian army corps under Prince Bagratian before Mohilew; on July 25, a bloody battle was fought near Ostrowno. The houses and other buildings of Ostrowno were filled with wounded, the battlefield covered with corpses of men and horses, and the hot weather caused quick putrefaction. Kerckhove visited the battlefield on June 28 and says:

> I have no words to describe the horror of seeing the unburied cadavers, infesting the air, and among the dead many helpless wounded without a drop of water, exposed to the hot sun, crying in rage and despair.

Napoleon made preparations to attack on July 28, but the enemy had retreated. At Witepsk, hospitals were established for the wounded from Ostrowno, among them 800 Russians. However, the designation "hospital" is hardly applicable, for everything was wanting; the patients in infected air, crowded, and surrounded by uncleanliness, without food or medicines. These hospitals were in reality death-houses. The physicians did what they could. On August 18, the French Army entered Smolensk which had been destroyed by projectiles and by fire; ruins filled with the dead and dying; and in the midst of this desolation the terror-stricken inhabitants running everywhere, looking for members of their families—many of whom had been killed by bullets or by flames—or sitting before their still smoking homes, tearing their hair, a picture of distress truly heartrending. The soldiers who were the first to enter Smolensk found flour, brandy and wine, but these things were devoured in an instant. There were ten thousand wounded in the so-called hospitals, and among these unfortunates typhus and hospital gangrene developed rapidly; the sick lying on the floor without even straw.

Holzhausen gives the following description:

> After Smolensk had been evacuated by the Russians, most houses had been burnt out; the retreating Russians had destroyed everything that could be of any use. Corpses everywhere. Nobody had time to remove them, and the cannons, the freight wagons, the horses, and the infantry passed over them. On August 17th and 18th, was the Battle of Polotsk in which the Bavarians distinguished themselves. There were no medicines for the wounded, not even drinking water, no bread, no salt. Of the many unhealthy places in Russia this is the worst, it swarms with insects. Nostalgia was prevailing. They had a so-called dying chamber in the hospital for which the soldiers were longing, to rest there on straw, never to rise again.
>
> Awaiting their last the pious Bavarians repeated aloud their rosary, took refuge with the Jesuits, who had a convent at Polotsk, to receive the consolation of their religion.

Some thought Napoleon would rest here to establish the Polish kingdom. But this reasonable idea, if he had ever entertained it, he discarded. By giving his troops winter quarters, establishing magazines and hospitals he would have succeeded in subduing Russia by reinforcing his army; instead of all this he went on to Moscow without provisions, without magazines.

On August 30, the army reached Wiasma, a city of eight thousand or nine thousand inhabitants which had been set on fire upon the approach of the French. All the inhabitants had left. The soldiers fought the flames and saved some houses into which they brought those of their wounded and sick who could not drag themselves any farther. Cases of typhus were numerous. From Wiasma the army marched to Ghiat, a city of six thousand or seven thousand inhabitants; at this place Napoleon gave a two days' rest in order that the army could rally, clean their arms and prepare for battle (the Battle of Borodino on September 7. This battle is known under three names: the Russians have called it after the village of Borodino, of 200 inhabitants, near the battlefield and have now erected a monument there, a colonnade crowned with a cross; some historians have called it the battle of Moshaisk, after a nearby town of four thousand inhabitants, and Napoleon has named it the Battle of the Moskwa, after a river near the battlefield.)

Napoleon had only 120 thousand to 130 thousand under arms, about as many as the Russians. It was 6:30 a.m., a beautiful sunrise. Napoleon called it the sun of Austerlitz. The Russian generals made their soldiers say their prayers. A French cannon gave the signal to attack, and at once the French batteries opened the battle with a discharge of more than 100 cannon. Writing this medical history of the Russian campaign I feel tempted to give a description of this most frightful, most cruel of all battles in the history of the world in which about 1,200 cannon without interruption dealt destruction and death; fracas and tumult of arms of all kinds, the harangue, the shouts of the commanders, the cries of rage, the lamentations of the wounded, all blended into one terrible din. Both armies charged with all the force that terror could develop. French and Russian soldiers not only fought like furious lions rivalling each other in ardour and courage, but they fought with wild joy, devoid of all human feeling, like maniacs; they threw themselves on the enemy where he was most numerous, in a manner which manifested the highest degree of despair.

The French had to gain the victory or succumb to misery; victory or death was their only thought. The Russians felt themselves humiliated by the approach of the French to their capital, and unshaken as a rock they resisted, defending themselves with grim determination. The battle, Napoleon promised, would be followed by peace and good winter quarters, but he was not as good a prophet as he was a good general.

During the day the Westphalian corps was reduced to 1500 men. Napoleon ordered these to do guard-duty on the battlefield, transport the immense number of wounded to the hospitals, bury the dead and to remain while the army marched and stayed at Moscow. What the Westphalians could do for the wounded was very little, for everything was wanting. The hospital system was incomplete, miserable. It is true, the surgeons dressed, operated, amputated, during the battle and during the days following, a great many wounded, but their number and their assistance was inadequate for the enormous task; thousands remained without proper attendance and died.

About one thousand Wuerttembergians were wounded in the Battle of Borodino, and on many of these surgical operations had to be performed. Strange to say, the greatest operations on enfeebled wounded were more successful, a great many more were saved, than was generally the case under more favourable circumstances. Thus Surgeon General von Kohlreuter observed that in the Russian campaign amputation of an arm, for instance, gave much better chances, more recoveries, than in the Saxon and French campaigns, during which latter the soldiers were still robust, well nourished and well, even in abundance, supplied with everything.

Means of transportation were lacking, for no wagons could be found in the deserted villages, and for this reason many whose wounds had been dressed had to be left to their fate—to die. Those but slightly wounded and those even who could crawl in some manner followed the troops, or went back at random to find their death in some miserable hut. Many sought refuge in nearby villages, sometimes miles away from the battle-field, there to fall into the hands of the Cossacks.

The Westphalians remained on the battlefield surrounded by corpses and dying men, and they were forced to change position from time to time on account of the stench. The scenes of suffering and distress which the battlefield presented everywhere surpassed all description; the groans of the mutilated and dying followed the men on guard even at a distance, and especially was this terrible during the night; it filled the heart with horror, von Borcke said that soldiers, at the request of some of the wounded in extreme agony, shot them dead and turned the face away while shooting. And soon they considered this an act of pity. The officers even induced them to look for those who could not be saved, in order to relieve them from their suffering. When von Borcke was riding on horseback over the battlefield on the 5th day after the battle he saw wounded soldiers lying alongside the cadaver of a horse, gnawing at its flesh. During the night flames could be seen here and there on this field of death; these were fires built by wounded soldiers who had crawled together to protect themselves from the cold of the night and to roast a piece of horseflesh. On September 12th the Westphalians moved to Moshaisk, which was deserted by all inhabitants, plundered, and half in ashes. While the battle raged several thousand wounded Russians had taken refuge there, who now, some alive and some dead, filled all the houses of the town. Burnt bodies were lying in the ruins of the houses which had been burnt, the entrance of these places being almost blockaded by cadavers.

The only church, which stood on the public square in the middle of the town, contained several hundred wounded and as many corpses of men dead for a number of days. One glance into this infected church, a regular pest-house, made the blood curdle. Surgeons went inside and had the dead piled up on the square around the church; those still alive and suffering received the first aid, order was established and gradually a hospital arranged. Soldiers, Westphalians as well as Russian prisoners, were ordered to remove the corpses from the houses and the streets, and then a recleansing of the whole town was necessary before it could be occupied by the troops. Although there was only one stone building—and a hundred wooden ones—it gave quarters to the whole Westphalian corps. Two regiments, one of Hussars, the other of the light Horse Guards, both together numbering not more than 300 men, had taken possession of a monastery in the neighbourhood. Two regiments of cuirassiers had marched with the French to Moscow.

In the quarters of Moshaisk the Westphalians enjoyed a time of rest, while the events in Moscow took place. The fate of those who had remained in Moshaisk was not enviable, but what had been left of the town offered at least shelter during the cold nights of the approaching winter. This was a good deal after the fearful hardships, and it contributed much toward the recuperation of the soldiers. Convalescents arrived daily, also such as had remained in the rear; a number of the slightly wounded were able for duty again, and in this manner the number of men increased to 4,500. Life in Moshaisk was a constant struggle for sustenance. There were no inhabitants, not even a single dog or any other living animal which the inhabitants had left behind. Some provisions found in houses or hidden somewhere benefitted only those who had discovered them. The place upon the whole was a desert for the hungry. Small detachments had to be sent out for supplies.

At first this system proved satisfactory, and with what had been brought in from the vicinity regular rations could be distributed. But the instinct of self-preservation had become so predominating that everyone thought only of himself. Officers would send men clandestinely for their own sake, and when this was discovered it ended in a fight and murder. Everyone was anxious to provide for himself individually, to be prepared for the coming winter. Sutlers and speculators went to Moscow to take advantage of the general pillage, to procure luxuries, like coffee, sugar, tea, wine, delicacies of all description. Notwithstanding the great conflagration at Moscow immense stores of all these things had come into the hands of the French, and this had an influence on Moshaisk, forty miles away from the metropolis, von Borcke was fortunate enough to secure a supply of coffee, tea, and sugar, sufficient not only for himself, but also for some friends, and lasting even for some weeks on the retreat. But the supply of meat, and especially bread, was inadequate for the mass of soldiers. Ten days had elapsed when the situation of those in Moshaisk became grave again, namely, when communication with Moscow was cut off. Orderlies did not arrive, no more convalescents came, news could not be had, details of soldiers sent out for supplies were killed or taken prisoner by Cossacks. The retreat of the French army, the last act of the great drama, commenced.

While the Westphalians guarded the battlefield the army marched to Moscow, exhausted, starving, finding new sufferings every day. On the road from Moshaisk to Moscow they encountered frightful conditions in the villages which were filled with wounded Russians. These unfortunates, abandoned to cruel privations, dying as much from starvation as from their wounds, excited pity. The water even was scarce, and when a source was discovered it was generally polluted, soiled with all sorts of filth, infected by cadavers; but all this did not prevent the soldiers from drinking it with great avidity, and they fought among themselves to approach it. All these details have to be known before studying typhus in the grand army.

★★★★★★

The description of diseases given by the physicians who lived a century ago is for us unsatisfactory; we cannot understand what they meant by their vague designating of hepatitis, fibrous enteritis, diarrhoea and dysentery, peripneumonia, remittent and intermittent gastric fever, protracted nervous fever, typhus and synochus; there is no distinction made in any of the writings of that period between abdominal and exanthematic typhus.

However, before long physicians will discard much from our present medical onomatology that is ridiculous, absurd, incorrect, in short, unscientific, as, for instance, the designation typhoid fever.

Ebstein has pointed out all that is obscure to us in the reports of the physicians of the Russian campaign; for instance, that we cannot distinguish what is meant by the different forms of fever. According to the views of those times fever was itself a disease *per se*; when reaction was predominating it was called *synocha*, typhus when weakness was the feature, and in case of a combination of *synocha* and typhus it was called *synochus*, a form in which there was at first an inflammatory and later on a typhoid stage, but which form could not be distinguished exactly from typhus. From all the descriptions in the reports of the Russian campaign it can be deduced that many of the cases enumerated were of exanthematic typhus, notwithstanding that the symptomatology given is very incomplete, not to speak of the pathological anatomy.

The only writer who has described necropsies is von Scherer. Some of the physicians speak only of the sick and the diseases, as Bourgeois, who says that on the march to Russia during the sultry weather the many cadavers of horses putrefied rapidly, filling the air with miasms, and that this caused much disease; further, in describing the retreat he only says that the army was daily reduced in consequence of the constant fighting, the privations and diseases, without enumerating which diseases were prevailing; only in a note attached to his booklet he mentions that the most frequent of the ravaging diseases of that time and during the Russian campaign in general was typhus, and there can be no doubt it was petechial or exanthematic typhus, for which the English literature has the vague name typhus fever.

Very interesting are the historical data given by Ebstein:

> As is well known, the fourth and most severe typhus period of the eighteenth century began with the wars of the French revolution and ended only during the second decade of the nineteenth century with the downfall of the Napoleonic empire and the restoration of peace in Germany.

During the Russian campaign the conditions for spreading the disease were certainly the most favourable imaginable.

Krantz, whom I shall quote later on, has described the ophthalmy prevailing in York's corps as being of a mild character.

Quite different forms reigned among the soldiers on their retreat from Moscow.

The description of the death from frost given by von Scherer is similar to that given by Bourgeois. The men staggered as if drunk, their faces were red and swollen, it looked as if all their blood had risen into their head. Powerless they dropped, as if paralyzed, the arms were hanging down, the musket fell out of their hands. The moment they lost their strength tears came to their eyes, repeatedly they arose, apparently deprived of their senses, and stared shy and terror-stricken at their surroundings. The physiognomy, the spasmodic contractions of the muscles of the face, manifested the cruel agony which they suffered. The eyes were very red, and drops of blood trickled from the conjunctiva. Without exaggeration it could be said of these unfortunates that they shed bloody tears. These severe forms of ophthalmy caused by extreme cold would have ended in gangrene of the affected parts if death had not relieved the misery of these unfortunates.

But Bourgeois describes another very severe form of ophthalmy among the soldiers which caused total blindness. It appeared when the army on its retreat was in the vicinity of Orscha, attacked many soldiers and resembled the ophthalmy which was prevailing in Egypt; there it was caused by the heated sand reflecting powerfully the rays of the sun; here, by the glaring white snow likewise reflecting the rays of the sun. Bourgeois considers as predisposing moments the smoke of the camp-fires, the want of sleep, the marching during the night, and describes the affection as follows: The conjunctiva became dark red, swelled together with the eyelids; there was a greatly exaggerated lachrymal secretion associated with severe pain; the eyes were constantly wet, the photophobia reached such a degree that the men became totally blind, suffered most excruciating pain and fell on the road.

Ebstein availed himself of the publications of J. L. R. de Kerckhove, Réné Bourgeois, J. Lemazurier, and Joh. von Scherer, and the manuscript of Harnier from which writings he collected all that refers to the diseases of the grand army. It may not be out of place to quote the interesting writings of de Kerckhove concerning the army physicians and Napoleon and his soldiers:

De Kerckhove left Mayence on March 6th, 1812, attached to the headquarters of the 3rd corps, commanded by Ney; at Thorn he joined those braves with whom he entered Moscow on September 14th and with whom he left on October 19th. When he returned to Berlin in the beginning of February, 1813, the 3rd corps was discharged. He writes:

The army was not only the most beautiful, but there was none which included so many brave warriors, more heroes. How many parents have cried over the loss of their children tenderly raised by them, how many sons, the only hope and support of their father and mother, have perished, how many bonds of friendship have been severed, how many couples have been separated forever, how many unfortunate ones drawn into misery? An army extinguished by hunger and cold!

Giving credit to the physicians and surgeons who took part in that unfortunate expedition he says:

With what noble zeal they tried to do their duties. The horror of the privations, the severity of the climate and fatigues and the want of eatables and medicines which characterized the hospitals and ambulances in Russia, have not discouraged the physicians so far as to become indifferent to the terrible fate reserved for the sick. On the contrary, far from allowing themselves to relax, they have doubled their activity to ameliorate sufferings. We have seen physicians in the midst of the carnage and the terror of the battles extend their care and bring consolation; we have seen them sacrificing day and night in hospital service, succumbing to murderous epidemics; in one word, despising all danger when it was a question of relieving the sufferings of the warriors, immaterial whether Russian or French. We can speak of many sick or wounded left in ambulances or hospitals in want of food and medicines, many of such unfortunates deprived of everything, dragging themselves under the ruins of cities or villages, who found help from honest physicians.

The Grand Army in Moscow

Three fifths of the houses and one half of the churches were destroyed. The citizens had burned their capital. Before this catastrophe of 1812 Moscow was an aristocratic city. According to old usage, the Russian nobility spent the winter there, they came from their country seats with hundreds of slaves and servants and many horses; their palaces in the city were surrounded by parks and lakes, and many buildings were erected on the grounds, as lodgings for the servants and slaves, stables, magazines. The number of servants was great, many of them serving for no other purpose than to increase the number, and this calling was part of the luxury of the noblemen. The house of the *seigneur* was sometimes of brick, rarely of stone, generally of wood, all were covered with copper plates or with iron, painted red or green. The magazines were mostly stone buildings, on account of the danger of fire.

At that time the Russian nobility had not yet accustomed itself to consider St. Petersburg the capital, they were obstinate in the determination to come every winter to hold court in the mother of Russian cities. The conflagration of 1812 broke this tradition. The nobility, not willing or not being able to rebuild their houses, rented the ground to citizens, and industry, prodigiously developing since then, has taken possession of Moscow. This is how the city has lost its floating population of noblemen and serfs, which amounted to 100 thousand souls, and how the aristocratic city has become an industrial one. It is a new city, but the fire of 1812, from the ashes of which it has risen, has left impressions on the monuments. Step by step in the Kremlin and in the city proper are found souvenirs of the patriotic war. You enter the Kremlin which Napoleon tried to explode, and which has been restored, you visit there the church of the Annunciation, and you will be told that the French soldiers had stabled their horses on the pavement of agate; you visit the church of the Assumption and you will be shown the treasures which, on the approach of the French, had been taken to places of safety; you raise your eye to the summit of the tower of Ivan and you learn that the cross had been removed by the invaders and found in the baggage of the Grand Army.

The door of St. Nicholas has an inscription recalling the miracle by which this door was saved in 1812. The tower surmounting it was split by an explosion from above downward, but the fissure ended at the very point where the icon is found; the explosion of 500 pounds of powder did not break even the glass which covers the image or the crystal of the lamp which burns before it. Along the walls of the arsenal are the cannon taken from the enemy, and in the arsenal are other trophies, including the camp-bed of Napoleon.

Russian accounts from eye-witnesses of the conflagration are few—in fact, there exists none in writing. People who witnessed the catastrophe could not write. What we possess are collections from verbal accounts given by servants, serfs, who had told the events to their masters. Nobody of distinction had remained in Moscow, none of the nobility, the clergy, the merchants. The persons from whom the following accounts are given were the nun Antonine, a former slave of the Syraxine family, the little peddler Andreas Alexieef, a woman, Alexandra Alexievna Nazarot, an old slave of the family Soimonof by the name of Basilli Ermolaevitch, the wife of a pope, Maria Stepanova, the wife of another pope, Helene Alexievna. A Russian lady has collected what she had learned from these humble people, the eye-witnesses of the catastrophe, and published it, pseudonym, in some Russian journal.

All these people had minutely narrated their experiences to her at great length, not omitting any detail which concerned themselves or circumstances which caused their surprise, and they all gave the dates, the hours which they had tenaciously kept in their memory for sixty years, for it was in the year 1872 when the Russian lady interrogated them. Some had retained from those days of terror such vivid impressions that a conflagration or the sight of a soldier's casque would cause them palpitation of the heart. There is much repetition in their narrations, for all had seen the same: the invasion, the enemy, the fire kindled by their own people, the misery, the dearth, the pillage. There exist documents of the events in Moscow of 1812, the souvenirs of Count de Toll, the apology of Rostopchine, which we shall come to in another chapter, the recitals of Domerque, of Wolzogen, of Ségur, but these reminiscences of people in Moscow are the only ones from persons who actually suffered by the catastrophe, and they are in their way as valuable as the writings of our two writers, von Scherer and von Borcke.

These plain people know nothing of the days of Erfurt, nothing of the continental *blocus*, nothing of the withdrawal of Alexander from the French Alliance; the bearers of the *toulloupes* (sheepskin furs) in the streets of Moscow of the beginning of 1812 knew nothing of the confederation of the Rhine; all they knew of Bonaparte was that he had often beaten the Germans, and that on his account they had to pay more for sugar and coffee. To them the great comet of 1811 was the first announcement of coming great events. Let us see the reflections which the comet inspired in the abbess of the Devitchi convent and the nun Antonine, and this will give us an idea of the mental condition of the latter, one of the narrators. She relates:

One evening, we were at service in St. John's church, when all of a sudden I noticed on the horizon a gerbe of resplendent flames. I cried out and dropped my lantern. Mother abbess came to me to learn what had caused my fright, and when she also had seen the meteor she contemplated a long time. I asked, Matouchka, what star is this? She answered this is no star, this is a comet. I asked again what is a comet? I never had heard that word. The mother then explained to me that this was a sign from heaven which God had sent to foretell great misfortune. Every evening this comet was seen, and we asked ourselves what calamity this one might bring us. In the cells of the convent, in the shops of the city, the news, travelling as the crow flies, was heard that Bonaparte was leading against Russia an immense army, the like of which the world had never seen.

Only the veterans of the battles of Austerlitz, Eylau, and Friedland could give some information, some details of the character of the invader. The direction which Napoleon took on his march left no doubt to any one that he would appear in Moscow. In order to raise the courage which was sinking they had the miraculous image of the Virgin *conductrice* brought from Smolensk, which place was to be visited by the French. This icon was exposed in the cathedral of St. Michael the Archangel, for veneration by the people. The abbess of our convent, who was from Smolensk, had a special devotion for this image, she went with all the nuns to salute the *Protatrix*.

At St. Michael the Archangel there was a great crowd so that one hardly could stand, especially were there many women, all crying. When we, the nuns, began to push, to get near the image, one after the other in a line endlessly long, they looked upon us with impatience. One woman said: 'These *soutanes* should make room for us, it is not their husbands, it is our husbands', our sons' heads, which will be exposed to the guns.'

Rostopchine tried his best to keep the population at peace by his original proclamations, which were pasted on all the walls and distributed broadcast. After Borodino he urged the people to take up arms, and he promised to be at the head of the men to fight a supreme battle on the Three Mountains. Meanwhile he worked to save the treasures of the church, the archives, the collections of precious objects in the government palaces. From the arsenal he armed the people. A tribune was erected from which the metropolitan addressed the multitude and made them kneel down to receive his blessing. Rostopchine stood behind the metropolitan and came forward after the priest had finished his elocution, saying that he had come to announce a great favour of his majesty. As a proof that they should not be delivered unarmed to the enemy, his majesty permitted them to pillage the arsenal, and the people shouted: "Thanks, may God give to the *Tzar* many years to live!" This was a very wise idea of Rostopchine to have the arsenal emptied, a feat which he could not have accomplished in time in any other way. The pillage lasted several days and went on in good order.

★★★★★★

The French had entered Moscow. The first word of Napoleon to Mortier, whom he had named governor of Moscow, was "no pillage!" But this point of honour had to be abandoned. The 100 thousand men who had entered were troops of the élite, but they came starving at the end of their adventurous expedition. During the first days they walked the streets in search of a piece of bread and a little wine. But little had been left in the cellars of the abandoned houses and in the basements of the little shops, and with the conflagration there was almost nothing to be found. The Grand Army was starving as much almost as on the march. Dogs which had returned in considerable numbers to lament on the ruins of the houses of their masters were looked upon as precious venison. The uniforms were already in rags, and the Russian climate made itself felt. These poor soldiers, poorly clad, dying from starvation, were begging for a piece of bread, for linen or sheepskin, and, above all, for shoes. There was no arrangement for the distribution of rations; they had to take from wherever they could, or perish.

Napoleon established himself in the Kremlin, the generals in the mansions of the noblemen, the soldiers in the taverns or private houses until the fire dislodged them. Napoleon, with a part of his staff, was obliged to seek refuge in the park Petrovski, the commanders took quarters wherever they could, the soldiers dispersed themselves among the ruins. Supervision had become an impossibility. The men, left to themselves, naturally lost all discipline under these circumstances of deception and under so many provocations among a hostile population. Notwithstanding all these conditions, they behaved well in general and to a great extent showed self-control and humanity toward the conquered. The example of pillage had been set by the Russians themselves. Koutouzof had commanded the destruction of the mansions. The slaves burned the palaces of their masters.

All eye-witnesses speak of the extreme destitution of the soldiers in regard to clothing after one month's stay in Moscow. Already at this time, even before the most terrible and final trials of the retreat which awaited them, one had to consider them lost. When they first took to woman's clothes or shoes or hats it was considered an amusement, a joke, but very soon a *mantilla*, a *soutane*, a veil became a precious object and nobody laughed at it when frozen members were wrapped in these garments. The greatest calamity was the want of shoes. Some soldiers followed women simply for the purpose of taking their shoes from them. A special chapter of horrors could be written on the sufferings of the soldiers on the retreat over ice and snow fields on account of the miserable supply of shoes.

At first Napoleon reviewed the regiments near the ponds of the Kremlin, and at the first reviews the troops marched proudly, briskly, with firm step, but soon they began to fail with astonishing rapidity. They answered the roll of the drums calling them together, clad in dirty rags and with torn shoes, in fast diminishing numbers. During the last weeks of their stay in Moscow many had reached the last stage of misery, after having wandered through the streets looking for a little bit of nourishment, dressed up as for a carnival, but without desire to dance, as one remarked in grim humour.

These were the men whose destination had brought them many hundreds of miles from home to the semi-Asiatic capital of the Ivans, who had been drinking in the glory and the joy of warriors, and who now died from hunger and cold, with their laurels still intact. Thanks to the authorized military requisitions and the excesses of the stragglers of the Grand Army, a desert had been made of the city before Napoleon had begun his retreat. No more cattle, no provisions, and the inhabitants gone, camping with wife and children in the deepest parts of the forests. Those who had remained or returned to the villages, organized against marauders whom they received with pitchforks or rifles, and these peasants gave no quarter. Maria Stepanova, the wife of a pope says:

> The enemy appeared nearly every day in our village (Bogorodsic), and as soon as they were perceived all men took up arms; our Cossacks charged them with their long sabres or shot them with their pistols, and behind the Cossacks were running the peasants, some with axes, some with pitchforks. After every excursion they brought ten or more prisoners which they drowned in the Protka which runs near the village, or they fusilladed them on the prairie. The unfortunates passed our windows, my mother and I did not know where to hide ourselves in order not to hear their cries and the report of the firearms. My poor husband, Ivan Demitovitch, became quite pale, the fever took him, his teeth chattered, he was so compassionate! One day the Cossacks brought some prisoners and locked them up in a cart-house built of stone. They are too few, they said, it is not worthwhile to take any trouble about them now; with the next lot which we shall take we will shoot or drown them together. This cart-house had a window with bars. Peasants came to look at the prisoners and gave them bread and boiled eggs; they did not want to see them starving while awaiting death. One day when I brought them eatables I saw at the window a young soldier—so young! His forehead was pressed against the bars, tears in his eyes, and tears running down his cheeks. I myself began to cry, and even today my heart aches when I think of him. I passed *lepecheks* through the bars and went away without looking behind me. At that time came an order from the government that no more prisoners should be killed but sent to Kalouga. How we were contented!"

Many savageries have been committed by the low class of Russians who had remained in Moscow. This is not surprising because these were of the most depraved of the population, including especially many criminals who had been set free to pillage and burn the city. "A little while before the French entered," tells the serf Soimonof, "the order had been given to empty all the vodka (whiskey) from the distilleries of the crown into the street; the liquor was running in rivulets, and the rabble drank until they were senselessly drunk, they had even licked the stones and the wooden pavement. Shouting and fighting naturally followed."

The really good people of Moscow had given proofs of high moral qualities, worthy of admiration, under the sad circumstances. Poor *moujiks* who had learned of the defeat of the Russians at Borodino said their place was no longer in a city which was to be desecrated by the presence of the enemy, and, leaving their huts to be burned down, their miserable belongings to be pillaged, they went on the highways at the mercy of God, disposed to march as long as their eyes could see before them. Others, running before the flames, carried their aged and sick on their shoulders, showing but one sentiment in their complete ruin, namely, absolute resignation to the will of God.

Some readers may say that the foregoing chapter does not give the medical history of the campaign. To these I wish to reply that it is impossible to understand the medical history without knowing the general conditions of the Grand Army, which were the cause of the death of hundreds of thousands of soldiers from cold and starvation.

Rostopchine

The conflagration of Moscow in 1812 and the fall of the French empire are two facts which cannot be separated, but to the name of Moscow is attached another name, that of Rostopchine. Count Fedor Wassiljavitch Rostopchine is connected with one of the greatest events in universal history. He caused a crisis which decided the fate of Russia and arrested the march of ascending France by giving the death blow to Napoleon. The latter, in admitting that Rostopchine was the author of his ruin, meant him when he said, "one man less, and I would have been master of the world."

Until the year 1876 there existed a mystery around this man and his deed, a mystery which was deepened by Rostopchine himself when he published in 1823 a pamphlet entitled *The Truth about the Conflagration of Moscow*, which did not give the truth but was a mystification.

Alexander Popof, a Russian Counsellor of State, who made a special study of the history of the Russian campaign of Napoleon, has explored the archives of St. Petersburg, and his researches, the result of which he published in Russian in the year 1876, have brought to light all diplomacy had concealed about the events which led to the destruction of the Russian capital.

What document, one might ask, could be more precious than the memoirs of Rostopchine, the governor of Moscow in 1812? What good fortune for the historian! In 1872 Count Anatole de Ségur, grandson of Rostopchine, the author of a biography of the latter, wrote, concerning these memoirs, that they were seized, together with all the papers of his grand-father, by order of the Emperor Nicholas, immediately after Rostopchine's death in the year 1826, and were locked up in the archives of the Imperial Chancellor where they would remain, perhaps forever. Fortunately, one of the daughters of Count Rostopchine had taken a copy of some passages of this precious manuscript. These passages were published in 1864 by a son of Rostopchine, Count Alexis R., in a book entitled *Materiaux en grande partie inédits, pour la biographie future du Comte Rostopchine*, which is of a rare bibliographic value, for only twelve copies were printed. These same fragments, three in number, were reproduced by Count Anatole de Ségur in the biography of his ancestor, of which we have spoken. Aside from these extracts nothing was known of Rostopchine's memoirs until Popof had made his researches. To verify the memoirs Popof quotes long passages which he compares carefully with other documents of that epoch. This book on the whole is a continuous commentary upon the memoirs of Rostopchine.

Rostopchine, having been made governor of Moscow in March, 1812, wrote to the *Tzar*:

Your empire has two strongholds, its immensity and its climate. It has these 16,000,000 men who profess the same creed, speak the same language, and whose chin has never been touched by a razor. The long beards are the power of Russia, and the blood of your soldiers will be a seed of heroes. If unfortunate circumstances should force you to retreat before the invader, the Russian emperor will always be terrible in Moscow, formidable in Kazan, invincible at Tobolsk.

This letter was dated June 11/23, 1812.

At that time Rostopchine was 47 years of age, in perfect health and had developed a most extraordinary activity, something which was not known of his predecessors; the governors of Moscow before his time had been old and decrepit. He understood the character of the Russian people and made himself popular at once, and adored, because he made himself accessible to everybody. He himself describes how he went to work:

I announced that every day from 11 to noon everybody had access to me, and those who had something important to communicate would be received at any hour during the day. On the day of my taking charge I had prayers said and candles lighted before such miraculous pictures as enjoyed the highest popular veneration. I studied to show an extraordinary politeness to all who had dealings with me; I courted the old women, the babblers and the pious, especially the latter. I resorted to all means to make myself agreeable; I had the coffins raised which served as signs to the undertakers and the inscriptions pasted on the

46

church doors. It took me two days to pull the wool over their eyes (*pour jeter la poudre aux yeux*) and to persuade the greater part of the inhabitants that I was indefatigable and that I was everywhere.

I succeeded in giving this idea by appearing on the same morning at different places, far apart from each other, leaving traces everywhere of my justice and severity; thus on the first day I had arrested an officer of the military hospital whose duty it was to oversee the distribution of the soup, but who had not been present when it was time for dinner. I rendered justice to a peasant who had bought 30 pounds of salt but received only 25; I gave the order to imprison an employee who had not done his duty; I went everywhere, spoke to everyone and learned many things which afterward were useful to me. After having tired to death two pairs of horses I came home at 8 o'clock, changed my civilian costume for the military uniform and made myself ready to commence my official work.

Thus Rostopchine took the Moscovitians by their foibles, played the *rôle* of Haroun-al-Raschid, played comedy; he even employed agents to carry the news of the town to him, to canvass war news and to excite enthusiasm in the cafés and in all kinds of resorts of the common people.

When the emperor notified him one day of his coming visit to the capital and transmitted a proclamation in which he announced to his people the danger of the country, Rostopchine developed great activity. He writes in his memoirs:

I went to work, was on my feet day and night, held meetings, saw many people, had printed along with the imperial proclamation a bulletin worded after my own fashion, and the next morning the people of Moscow on rising learned of the coming of the sovereign. The nobility felt flattered on account of the confidence which the emperor placed in them, and became inspired with a noble zeal, the merchants were ready to give money, only the common people apparently remained indifferent, because they did not believe it possible that the enemy could enter Moscow.

The longbeards repeated incessantly:

"Napoleon cannot conquer us, he would have to exterminate us all."

But the streets became crowded with people, the stores were closed, everyone went first to the churches to pray for the *Tzar*, and from there to the gate of Dragomilof to salute the imperial procession upon its arrival. The enthusiasm ran so high that the idea was conceived to unhitch the horses from his coach and carry him in his carriage. This, as Rostopchine tells us, was the intention not only of the common people but of many distinguished ones also, even of such as wore decorations. The emperor, to avoid such exaggerated manifestations, was obliged to arrange for his entry during the night. On the next morning when the *Tzar*, according to the old custom, showed himself to his people on the red stairs, the hurrahs, the shouts of the multitude drowned the sounds of the bells of the forty times forty churches which were ringing in the city. At every step, thousands of hands tried to touch the limbs of the sovereign or the flap of his uniform which they kissed and wet with their tears. Rostopchine writes:

I learned during the night, and it was confirmed in the morning, that there were some persons who had united to ask the emperor how many troops we had, how many the enemy, and what were the means of defence. This would have been a bold and, under the present circumstances, a dangerous undertaking, although I hardly feared that these people would venture to do so, because they were of those who are brave in private and poltroons in public.

At any rate, I had said repeatedly and before everybody that I hoped to offer the emperor the spectacle of an assembly of a faithful and respectful nobility, and that I should be in despair if some malevolent person should permit himself to create disorder and forget the presence of the sovereign. I promised that anyone who would do this might be sure of being taken in hand and sent on a long journey before he would have finished his harangue.

To give more weight to my words I had stationed, not far from the palace, two *telegues* (two-wheeled carts) hitched up with mail horses and two police officers in road uniform promenading before them. If some curious person should ask them for whom these *telegues* were ready, they had orders to answer, 'for those who will be sent to Siberia.'

These answers and the news of the *telegues* soon spread among the assembly; the bawlers understood and behaved.

The nobility of Riazen had sent a deputation to the emperor to offer him sixty thousand men, armed and equipped. Balachef, the minister of police, received this deputation scornfully and ordered them to leave Moscow at once.

There were other offers which were not surprising at that period when the mass of the people consisted of serfs, but which appear strange to us. Kamarovski writes:

> Many of my acquaintances said that they would give their musicians, others the actors of their theatres, others their hunters, as it was easier to make soldiers of them than of their peasants.

The Russian noblemen in their love for liberty sacrificed their slaves. Rostopchine, together with many aristocrats, was not entirely at ease. It was something anomalous to call to arms for the sake of liberty a nation of serfs who vividly felt the injustice of their situation; besides, it had been heard that some *moujiks* said, "Bonaparte comes to bring us liberty, we do not want any more *seigneurs*."

The Russian people in their generality, however, did not justify the fears of the aristocrats. Their religious fanaticism, nourished by the priests, their passionate devotion to the *Tzar*, made them forget their own, just complaints.

In Moscow business was at a standstill, the ordinary course of things was likewise suspended, the population lived in the streets, forming a nervous crowd, subject to excitement and terror. The question was to keep them in respectfulness.

Here Rostopchine's inborn talent as tribune and publicist, as comedian and tragedian, showed itself to perfection. He gave a free rein to his imagination in his placards, in which he affected the proverbial language of the *moujik*, made himself a peasant, more than a peasant, in his eccentric style, to excite patriotism. He published pamphlets against the French, and the coarser his language the more effect it had on the masses. He writes:

> At this time I understood the necessity of acting on the mind of the people to arouse them so that they should prepare themselves for all the sacrifices, for the sake of the country. Every day I disseminated stories and caricatures, which represented the French as dwarfs in rags, poorly armed, not heavier than a gerbe which one could lift with a pitchfork.

For curiosity's sake, as an example of his style of fiction by which he fascinated the Russian peasantry may serve the translation of one of the stories:

Korniouchka Tchikhirine, an inhabitant of Moscow, a veteran, having been drinking a little more than usual, hears that Bonaparte is coming to Moscow, he becomes angry, scolds in coarse terms all Frenchmen, comes out of the liquor store and under the eagle with the two heads (the sign that the place is the crown's) he shouts: What, he will come to us! But you are welcome! For Christmas or carnival you are invited. The girls await you with knots in their handkerchiefs, your head will swell. You will do well to dress as the devil; we shall say a prayer, and you will disappear when the cock crows. Do better, remain at home, play hide and seek or blind man's buff. Enough of such farces! don't you see that your soldiers are cripples, dandies? They have no *touloupes*, no mittens, no *onoutchi* (wrappings around the legs in place of stockings). How will they adapt themselves to Russian habits? The cabbage will make them bloated, the gruel will make them sick, and those who survive the winter will perish by the frost at Epiphany. So it is, yes.

At our house doors they will shiver, in the vestibule they will stand with chattering teeth; in the room they will suffocate, on the stove they will be roasted. But what is the use of speaking? As often as the pitcher goes to the well, as often their head will be broken. Charles of Sweden was another imprudent one like you, of pure royal blood, he has gone to Poltava, he has not returned. Other rabbits than you Frenchmen were the Poles, the Tartars, the Swedes; our forefathers, however, have dealt with them so that one can yet see the tomb-hills around Moscow, as numerous as mushrooms, and under these mushrooms rest their bones. Ah! our holy mother Moscow, it is not a city, it is an empire. You have left at home only the blind and the lame, the old women and the little children.

Your size is not big enough to match the Germans; they will at the first blow throw you on your back (this remark is wonderfully prophetic). And Russia, do you know what that is, you cracked head? Six hundred thousand longbeards have been enlisted, besides 300 thousand soldiers with bare chins, and 200 thousand veterans. All these are heroes; they believe in one God, obey one *Tzar*, make the sign with one cross, these are all brethren. And if it pleases our father and *Tzar*, Alexander Pavlovitch, he has to say only one word: To arms, Christians! And you will see them rising. And even if you should beat the vanguard? Take your ease! the others will give you such a chase that the memory of it will remain in all eternity. To come to us! well then!

Not only the tower of Ivan the Great, but also the hill of Prosternations will remain invisible to you even in your dream. We shall rely on white Russia and we shall bury you in Poland. As one makes his bed so one sleeps. On this account reflect, do not proceed, do not start the dance. Turn about face, go home, and from generation to generation remember what it is, the Russian nation. Having said all, Tchikhirine went on, briskly singing, and the people who saw him go said wherever he came, that is well spoken, it is the truth!''

Rostopchine knew very well how to make Tchikhirine speak when he had been drinking more than usual, he knew how to make the saints speak, he invented pious legends which were not guaranteed by the Holy Synod and not found in the Lives of the Saints. He said in his memoirs:

> After the Battle of Borodino, I ceased to have recourse to little means to distract the people and occupy their attention. It required an extraordinary effort of the imagination to invent something that would excite the people. The most ingenious attempts do not always succeed, while the clumsy ones take a surprising effect. Among those of the latter kind there was a story after my fashion of which five thousand copies at one *kopek* a copy were sold in one day.

The population of Moscow was in a peculiar moral condition. They were most superstitious, believed the most improbable reports and saw signs from heaven of the downfall of Napoleon. Rostopchine writes:

> In the city rumours were current of visions, of voices which had been heard in the graveyards. Passages from the *Apocalypsis* were quoted referring to Napoleon's fall.

But Rostopchine himself, was he free from credulity? A German by the name of Leppich constructed, secretly, in one of the gardens of Moscow, a balloon by means of which the French army should be covered with fire, and some historians say that Rostopchine was one of the most enthusiastic admirers of Leppich.

As it may be interesting to learn how he was ahead of his time in regard to ideas about military balloons let us give the full statement of Popof on this matter.

In 1812 in Moscow it was exactly as in 1870 in Paris; everybody built hopes on the military airship, and expected that by means of a Greek fire from a balloon the whole army of the enemy would be annihilated. Rostopchine, in a letter dated May 7/19, 1812, gave an account to Emperor Alexander of the precautions he had taken that the wonderful secret of the construction of the airship by Leppich should not be revealed. He took the precaution not to employ any workmen from Moscow. He had already given Leppich 120 thousand *rubles* to buy material. He writes:

> Tomorrow under the pretext of dining with someone living in his vicinity I shall go to Leppich and shall remain with him for a long time; it will be a feast to me to become more closely connected with a man whose invention will render military art superfluous, free mankind of its internal destroyer, make of you the arbiter of kings and empires and the benefactor of mankind.

In another letter to the emperor, dated June 11/23, 1812, he writes:

> I have seen Leppich; he is a very able man and an excellent mechanician. He has removed all my doubts in regard to the contrivances which set the wings of his machine in motion (indeed an infernal construction) and which consequently might do still more harm to humanity than Napoleon himself. I am in doubt about one point which I submit to the judgment of your majesty: when the machine will be ready Leppich proposes to embark on it to fly as far as Wilna. Can we trust him so completely as not to think of treason on his part?

Three weeks later he wrote to the emperor:

> I am fully convinced of success. I have taken quite a liking to Leppich who is also very much attached to me; his machine I love like my own child. Leppich suggests that I should make an air voyage with him, but I cannot decide about this without the authorization of your majesty.

On September 11th, four days before the evacuation, the fate of Moscow was decided. On that day at 10 o'clock in the forenoon the following conversation took place in the house of Rostopchine between him and Glinka.

"Your Excellency," said Glinka, "I have sent my family away."

"I have already done the same," answered the count, and tears were in his eyes.

"Now," added he, "Serge Nicholaevitch, let us speak like two true friends of our country. In your opinion, what will happen if Moscow is abandoned?"

"Your Excellency knows what I have dared to say on the 15/27 July in the assembly of the nobility; but tell me in all frankness, count, how shall Moscow be delivered, with blood, or without blood (*s kroviou ili bez krovi*)?"

"*Bez krovi* (without blood)," laconically answered the count.

His word to prince Eugene had been: Burn the capital rather than deliver it to the enemy; to Ermilof: I do not see why you take so much pains to defend Moscow at any price; if the enemy occupies the city he will find nothing that could serve him.

The treasures which belong to the crown and all that is of some value have already been removed; also, with few exceptions, the treasures of the churches, the ornaments of gold and silver, the most important archives of the state, all have been taken to a place of safety. Many of the well-to-do have already taken away what is precious. There remain in Moscow only fifty thousand persons in the most miserable conditions who have no other asylum.

This was what he said on September 13, and on the same day he wrote to the emperor that all had been sent away.

But this was not true; there still remained ten thousand wounded—of whom the majority would perish in case of a conflagration; there remained an immense stock of provisions, flour and alcoholic liquor, which would fall into the hands of the enemy; there was still the arsenal in the Kremlin containing 150 cannon, 60 thousand rifles, 160 thousand cartridges and a great deal of sulphur and saltpetre.

During the night from the 14th to the 15th Rostopchine developed a great activity, though he could save only some miraculous images left in the churches, and destroy some magazines.

The inhabitants suddenly aroused from their security went to the barriers of the city and obstructed the streets with vehicles; to remove what still remained in Moscow the means of transportation and the time allowed for this purpose were insufficient.

Those who remained had nothing to lose and were glad to take revenge on the rich by burning and pillaging their mansions.

On the 14th the criminals in the prisons, with one-half of their heads shaved, were set at liberty that they might participate in the burning and pillaging.

Before leaving Moscow Rostopchine uncovered his head and said to his son, "Salute Moscow for the last time; in half an hour it will be on fire."

Quite a literature has developed on the question: who has burned Moscow? The documents which Popof has examined leave no doubt concerning Rostopchine's part in regard to its conflagration. But, after all, it was caused by those who had a right to do it, those who, beginning at Smolensk, burned their villages, their hamlets, even their ripening or ripened harvest, after the Russian Army had passed and the enemy came in sight. Who? The Russian people of all classes, of all conditions without exception, men even invested with public power, and among them Rostopchine.

Retreat From Moscow

During the night from October 18th to October 19th, all soldiers were busy loading vehicles with provisions and baggage. On October 19th, the first day of the retreat, forever memorable on account of the misfortune and heroism which characterized it, the grand army presented a strange spectacle. The soldiers were in a fair condition, the horses lean and exhausted. But, above all, the masses following the army were extraordinary. After an immense train of artillery of 600 cannon, with all its supplies, came a train of baggage the like of which had never been seen since the centuries of migration when whole barbarous nations went in search of new territories for settlement.

The fear that they might run short of rations had caused every regiment, every battalion, to carry on country wagons all they had been able to procure of bread and flour; but these wagons carrying provisions were not the heaviest loaded, not loaded as much as those which were packed with booty from the conflagration of Moscow; in addition, many soldiers overtaxing their strength and endurance had filled their knapsacks with provisions and booty. Most officers had secured light Russian country wagons to carry provisions and warm clothing. The French, Italian, and German families, who lived in Moscow and now feared the returning Russians when again entering their capital, had asked to accompany the retreating army and formed a kind of a colony among the soldiers; with these families were also theatrical people and unfortunate women who had lived in Moscow on prostitution.

The almost endless number, the peculiarity of vehicles of all description, drawn by miserable horses, loaded with sacks of flour, clothing and furniture, with sick women and children, constituted a great danger, for the question was, how could the army manoeuvre with such an impediment and, above all, defend itself against the Cossacks?

Napoleon, surprised and almost alarmed, thought at first to establish order, but, after some reflection, came to the conclusion that the accidents of the road would soon reduce the quantity of this baggage, that it would be useless to be severe with the poor creatures, that, after all, the wagons would serve to transport the wounded. He consented therefore to let all go along the best they could, he only gave orders that the column of these people with their baggage should keep at a distance from the column of the soldiers in order that the army would be able to manoeuvre.

On October 24th was the Battle of Jaroslawetz in which the Russians, numbering twenty-four thousand, fought furiously against ten thousand or eleven thousand French, to cut off the latter from Kalouga, and the French, on their part, fought with despair.

The centre of the battle was the burning city taken and retaken seven times; many of the wounded perished in the flames, their cadavers incinerated, and ten thousand dead covered the battlefield.

Many of the wounded, who could not be transported had to be left to their fate at the theatre of their glorious devotion, to the great sorrow of everybody, and many who had been taken along on the march during the first days after the battle had also to be abandoned for want of means of transportation. The road was already covered with wagons for which there were no horses.

The cries of the wounded left on the road were heartrending, in vain did they implore their comrades not to let them die on the way, deprived of all aid, at the mercy of the Cossacks.

The artillery was rapidly declining on account of the exhausted condition of the horses. Notwithstanding all cursing and whipping, the jaded animals were not able to drag the heavy pieces. Cavalry horses were taken to overcome the difficulty and this caused a reduction of the strength of the cavalry regiments without being of much service to the artillery. The riders parted with their horses, they had tears in their eyes looking for the last time on their animals, but they did not utter a word.

Cavalrymen, with admirable perseverance and superhuman efforts, dragged the cannon as far as Krasnoe. All men had dismounted and aided the exhausted animals only two of which were attached to each piece.

Notwithstanding all the misery of a three-days-march to Moshaisk all were hopeful. The distance from Moshaisk to Smolensk was cov-

TRANSPORTATION OF CANON UNDER DIFFICULTIES

ered in seven or eight days; the weather, although cold during the night, was good during the day, and the soldiers gladly anticipated to find, after some more hardship, rest, abundance, and warm winter quarters in Smolensk.

On the march the army camped on the battlefield of Borodino when they saw fifty thousand cadavers lying still unburied, broken wagons, demolished cannons, helmets, *cuirasses*, guns spread all over—a horrid sight! Wherever the victims had fallen in large numbers one could see clouds of birds of prey rending the air with their sinister cries. The reflections which this sight excited were profoundly painful. How many victims, and what result! The army had marched from Wilna to Witebsk, from Witebsk to Smolensk, hoping for a decisive battle, seeking this battle at Wiasma, then at Ghjat, and had found it at last at Borodino, a bloody, terrible battle. The army had marched to Moscow in order to earn the fruit of all that sacrifice, and at this place nothing had been found but an immense conflagration. The army returned without magazines, reduced to a comparatively small number, with the prospect of a severe winter in Poland, and with a far away prospect of peace,—for peace could not be the price of a forced retreat,—and for such a result the field of Borodino was covered with fifty thousand dead. Here, as we have learned, were found the Westphalians, not more than three thousand, the remainder of 10 thousand at Smolensk, of twenty-three thousand who crossed the Niemen.

Napoleon gave orders to take the wounded at Borodino into the baggage wagons and forced every officer, every refugee from Moscow who had a vehicle, to take the wounded as the most precious load.

The rear guard under Davout left the fearful place on October 31st., and camped overnight halfway to the little town of Ghjat. The night was bitter cold, and the soldiers began to suffer very much from the low temperature.

From this time on, every day made the retreat more difficult, for the cold became more and more severe from day to day, and the enemy more pressing.

The Russian general, Kutusof, might now have marched ahead of Napoleon's army, which was retarded by so many impediments, and annihilated it by a decisive battle, but he did not take this risk, preferring a certain and safe tactic, by constantly harassing the French, surprising one or the other of the rear columns by a sudden attack. He had a strong force of cavalry and artillery, and, above all, good horses, while the rearguard of the French, for want of horses, consisted of infantry; there was, for instance, nothing left of General Grouchy's cavalry. The infantry of Marshal Davout, who commanded the rearguard, had to do the service of all arms, often being compelled to face the artillery of the enemy which had good horses, while their own was dragged along by exhausted animals scarcely able to move.

Davout's men fought the Russians with the bayonet and took cannons from them, but being without horses they were compelled to leave them on the road, content rearguarding themselves to remain undisturbed for some hours.

Gradually the French had to part with their own cannons and ammunition; sinister explosions told the soldiers of increasing distress.

As it is in all great calamities of great masses: increasing misery also increases egotism and heroism. Miserable drivers of wagons to whom the wounded had been entrusted took advantage of the night and threw the helpless wounded on the road where the rearguard found them dead or dying. The guilty drivers, when discovered, were punished; but it was difficult to detect them, with the general confusion of the retreat making its first appearance.

Wounded soldiers who had been abandoned could be seen at every step. The tail of the army, composed of stragglers, of tired, discouraged or sick soldiers, all marching without arms and without discipline, continually increased in number, to the mortification of the rearguard which had to deal with these men who would not subordinate their own selves to the welfare of the whole.

It is tempting to describe the terrible engagements, the almost superhuman, admirable bravery of Napoleon's soldiers, who often, after having had the hardest task imaginable and constantly in danger of being annihilated, were forced to pass the bitter cold nights without eating, without rest, and although all details bear on the medical history I am obliged to confine myself to a few sketches between the description of purely medical matters.

★★★★★★

I happened to find in the surgeon-general's library a rare book: Moricheau Beaupré, *A Treatise on the Effects and Properties of Cold, with a Sketch, Historical and Medical, of the Russian Campaign.* Translated by John Clendining, with appendix, xviii, 375 pp. 8vo., Edinburgh, Maclachnan and Stewart, 1826.

This most valuable book is not mentioned in any of the numerous publications on the medical history of the Russian campaign of Napoleon which I examined, and I shall now give an extract of what

Beaupré writes on the Effects of Cold in General:

Distant expeditions, immaterial whether in cold or warm countries, with extremes of temperature, are always disadvantageous and must cause great sacrifice of life, not only on account of the untried influence of extreme temperatures on individuals born in other climates, but also on account of the fatigues inseparable from traversing long distances, of an irregular life, of a multiplicity of events and circumstances impossible to foresee, or which at least had not been foreseen, and which operate very unfavourably, morally and physically, on military persons. The expedition of the French Army into Russia offers a sad proof of this truth, but history has recorded similar experiences. The army of Alexander the Great suffered frightfully from cold on two occasions: first, when that ambitious conqueror involved himself amid snows, in savage and barbarous regions of northern Asia before reaching the Caucasus; the second time, when, after having crossed these mountains, he passed the Tanais to subdue the Scythians, and the soldiers were oppressed with thirst, hunger, fatigue, and despair, so that a great number died on the road, or lost their feet from congelation; the cold seizing them, it benumbed their hands, and they fell at full length on the snow to rise no more.

The best means they knew, says Q. Curtius, to escape that mortal numbness, was not to stop, but to force themselves to keep marching, or else to light great fires at intervals. Charles XII, a great warrior alike rash and unreflecting, in 1707 penetrated into Russia and persisted in his determination of marching to Moscow despite the wise advice given him to retire into Poland. The winter was so severe and the cold so intense that the Swedes and Russians could scarcely hold their arms. He saw part of his army perish before his eyes, of cold, hunger, and misery, amid the desert and icy *steppes* of the Ukraine. If he had reached Moscow, it is probable that the Russians would have set him at bay, and that his army, forced to retire, would have experienced the same fate as the French.

In the retreat of Prague in 1742 the French Army, commanded by Marshal Belle-Isle, little accustomed to a winter campaign, was forced to traverse impracticable defiles across mountains and ravines covered with snow. In ten days four thousand men perished of cold and misery; food and clothing were deficient, the soldiers died in anguish and despair, and a great many of the officers and soldiers had their noses, feet and hands frozen. The Russians regard the winter of 1812 as one of the most rigorous of which they have any record; it was intensely felt through all Russia, even in the most southerly parts. As a proof of this fact the Tartars of the Crimea mentioned to Beaupré the behaviour of the great and little bustard, which annually at that season of the year quit the plain for protection against the cold and migrate to the southern part of that peninsula toward the coasts. But during that winter they were benumbed by the cold and dropped on the snow, so that a great many of them were caught. In the low hills, in the spring of 1813, the ground in some places was covered with the remains of those birds entire.

Of the effects of cold in general Beaupré says that soldiers who are rarely provided with certain articles of dress suitable for winter, whose caps do not entirely protect the lateral and superior parts of the head, and who often suffer from cold in bivouacs, are very liable to have ears and fingers seized on by asphyxia and mortification. Troopers who remain several days without taking off their boots, and whose usual posture on horseback contributes to benumb the extremities, often have their toes and feet frozen without suspecting it.

Cold produces fatal effects above as well as below the freezing point. A continued moderate cold has the same consequences as a severe cold of short duration. When very intense, as in the north, it sometimes acts on the organism so briskly as to depress and destroy its powers with astonishing rapidity. As the action of cold is most frequently slow and death does not take place until after several hours' exposure, the contraction that diminishes the calibre of the vessels more and more deeply, repels the blood toward the cavities of the head, chest, and abdomen; it causes, in the circulation of the lungs, and in that of the venous system of the head, an embarrassment that disturbs the function of the brain and concurs to produce somnolence. The probability of this explanation is strengthened by the flowing of the blood from the nose to the ears, spontaneous haemoptysis, also by preternatural redness of the viscera, engorgements of the cerebral vessel, and bloody effusion, all of which conditions have been found after death.

It is certain that in spite of every possible means of congestion or effusion within the cranium, constant and forced motion is necessary for the foot soldier to save him from surprise. The horseman must dismount as quickly as possible and constrain himself to walk. Commanders of divisions should not order halts in winter, and they should take care that the men do not lag behind on the march. Necessary above all are gaiety, courage, and perseverance of the mind; these qualities are the surest means of escaping danger. He who has the misfortune of being alone, inevitably perishes.

In Siberia, the Russian soldiers, to protect themselves from the action of the cold, cover their noses and ears with greased paper. Fatty matters seem to have the power of protecting from cold, or at least of greatly diminishing its action. The Laplander and the Samoiede anoint their skin with rancid fish oil, and thus expose themselves in the mountains to a temperature of -36 deg. Reaumur, or 50 deg. below zero Fahrenheit. Xenophon, during the retreat of the ten thousand, ordered all his soldiers to grease those parts that were exposed to the air. If this remedy could have been employed, says Beaupré, on the retreat from Moscow, it is probable that it would have prevented more than one accident.

Most of those who escaped the danger of the cold ultimately fell sick. In 1813 a number of soldiers, more or less seriously injured by cold, filled the hospitals of Poland, Prussia, and other parts of Germany. From the shores of the Niemen to the banks of the Rhine it was easy to recognize those persons who constituted the remainder of an army immolated by cold and misery the most appalling. Many, not yet arrived at the limit of their sufferings, distributed themselves in the hospitals on this side of the Rhine, and even as far as the south of France, where they came to undergo various extirpations, incisions, and amputations, necessitated by the physical disorder so often inseparable from profound gangrene.

Mutilation of hands and feet, loss of the nose, of an ear, weakness of sight, deafness, complete or incomplete, neuralgy, rheumatism, palsies, chronic diarrhoea, pectoral affections, recall still more strongly the horrors of this campaign to those who bear such painful mementos.

★★★★★★

But now let us return to the dissertation of von Scherer which gives the most graphic and complete description of the effect of cold.

After the Battle of Borodino, on September 5th and 7th, the army marched to Moscow and arrived there on September 11th, exhausted to the highest degree from hunger and misery. The number of Wuerttembergians suffering from dysentery was very large. A hospital was organized for them in a sugar refinery outside of Moscow. Many died here, but the greater number was left to its fate during the retreat of the army.

The quarters at Moscow until October 19th improved the condition of the army very little. Devoured by hunger, in want of all necessities, the army had arrived. The terrible fire of the immense city had greatly reduced the hope for comfortable winter quarters. Although the eatables which had been saved from the fire were distributed among the soldiers who, during the weeks of their sojourn, had wine, tea, coffee, meat, and bread, all wholesome and plentiful, yet dysentery continued and in most patients had assumed a typhoid character.[1] Besides, real typhus had now made its appearance in the army and, spreading rapidly through infection, caused great loss of life and brought the misery to a climax. The great number of the sick, crowded together in unfit quarters; the stench of the innumerable unburied and putrefying cadavers of men and animals in the streets of Moscow, among them the corpses of several thousand Russians who had been taken prisoners and then massacred, not to speak of the putrefying cadavers on the battlefields and roads over which the army had marched, all this had finally developed into a pest-like typhus.

After the retreat from Moscow had been decided upon, many thousands of the sick were sent ahead on wagons under strong guards. These wagons took the shortest road to Borodino, while the army took the road to Kaluga. Several thousand typhus patients were left in Moscow, all of whom died, with the exception of a few, according to later information. Many of those who, although suffering from typhus, had retained strength enough to have themselves transported on the wagons, recovered on the way, later to become victims of the cold.

Weakened in body and mind, the army left Moscow on October 18th and 19th. The weather was clear, the nights were cold, when they proceeded in forced marches on the road to Kaluga. Near Maloijorolawez the enemy attempted to bar the way, and an obstinate engagement developed during which the French cavalry suffered severely.

It is true, the Russian battle line was broken, and the way was open, but the French army had received its death-blow.

The order which thus far had kept the army was shaken, and disorder of all kinds commenced.

The retreat now continued in the direction of Borodino, Ghjat, and Wiasma, the same road which had been followed on the march

---

1. The word typhoid means "resembling typhus," and in Europe this term is correctly employed to designate a somnolent or other general condition in all kinds of feverish diseases which remind one of typhus symptoms. What English and American physicians call typhus or typhus fever is known to European physicians under the name of exanthematic or petechial typhus, indicating a symptom by which it is distinguished from abdominal typhus.

toward Moscow, a road which was laid waste and entirely deserted.

The soldiers, in view of the helplessness which manifested itself, gave up all hope and with dismay looked into a terrible future.

Everywhere surrounded by the enemy who attacked vehemently, the soldiers were forced to remain in their ranks on the highway; whoever straggled was lost—either killed or made prisoner of war.

On the immense tract of land extending from Moscow to Wilna during a march of several days, not a single inhabitant, not a head of cattle, was to be seen, only cities and villages burnt and in ruins. The misery increased from day to day. What little of provisions had been taken along from Moscow was lost, together with the wagons, on the flight after the engagement of Maloijorolawez, and this happened, as we have seen, before the army reached Borodino; the rations which the individual soldier had with him were consumed during the first few days, and thus a complete want made itself felt. The horses, receiving no food, fell in great numbers from exhaustion and starvation; cannon and innumerable wagons, for want of means to transport them, had to be destroyed and left behind.

From the last days of October until mid-December, at which time the army arrived at Wilna, horse meat was the only food of the soldiers; many could not obtain even this, and they died from starvation before the intense cold weather set in. The meat which the soldiers ate was either that of exhausted and sick horses which had not been able to walk any further, or of such as had been lying dead on the road for some time. With the greatest greed and a beastly rage the men threw themselves on the dead animals; they fought without distinction of rank and with a disregard of all military discipline—officers and privates alike—for the possession of the best liked parts of the dead animal—the brain, the heart, and the liver. The weakest had to be contented with any part. Many devoured the meat raw, others pierced it with the bayonet, roasted it at the camp fire and ate it without anything else, often with great relish.

Such was the sad condition when the setting in of extreme cold weather brought the misery—the horrors—to a climax.

During the last days of October, when the army had scarcely reached Borodino, cold winds blew from the North.

The first snowfall was on October 26th, and the snow made the march of the enfeebled army difficult in the extreme.

From that date on the cold increased daily, and the camping over night was terrible; the extremities of those who had no chance to protect themselves with clothes nor to come near the campfire became frozen.

During the first days of November the thermometer had fallen to -12 Reaumur (+4 Fahrenheit).

Derangements of mind were the first pernicious effects of the low temperature that were noticed.

The first effect on the brain in the strong and healthy ones, as well as in the others, was loss of memory.

Von Scherer noticed that, with the beginning of the cold weather, many could not remember the names of the best known, the everyday things, not even the eagerly longed for eatables could they name, or name correctly; many forgot their own names and were no longer able to recognize their nearest comrades and friends. Others had become completely feebleminded, their whole expression was that of stupidity. And those of a stronger constitution, who had resisted the effects of cold on body and mind, became deeply horrified on observing, in addition to their own sufferings, how the mental faculties of the best men, hitherto of strong will power, had become impaired, and how these unfortunates sooner or later, yet gradually, with lucid intervals of a few moments' duration, invariably became completely insane.

The intense cold enfeebled, first of all, the brain of those whose health had already suffered, especially of those who had had dysentery, but soon, while the cold increased daily, its pernicious effect was noticed in all.

The internal vessels, especially those of the brain and the lungs, in many became congested to such a degree that all vital activity was paralyzed.

On necropsy, these vessels of the brain and lungs and the right heart were found to be bloated and stretched; in one case the different vessels of the brain were torn and quite an amount of blood was effused between the meninges and the brain, in most cases more or less serum had collected in the cavities.

The corpses were white as snow, while the central organs in every case were hyperaemic.

At the beginning, while the cold was still tolerable, the effect of the humours from the surface of the body to the central organs had caused only a slight derangement of the functions of these organs, like dyspnoea, mental weakness, in some more or less indifference, a disregard of their surroundings; in short, all those symptoms of what was called at that time "Russian simpleton."

Now all actions of the afflicted manifested mental paralysis and the highest degree of apathy.

This condition resembles that of extreme old age, when mind and body return to the state of childhood.

The bodies of those suffering from intense cold were shrivelled and wrinkled. Men formerly models of bodily and mental strength, hardened in war, now staggered along, leaning on a stick, wailing and lamenting childlike, begging for a piece of bread, and if something to eat was given to them they burst out in really childish joy, not seldom shedding tears.

The faces of these unfortunates were deadly pale, the features strangely distorted. Lads resembled men of 80 years of age and presented a cretin-like appearance; the lips were bluish, the eyes dull, without lustre, and constantly lachrymal; the veins very small, scarcely visible; the extremities cold; the pulse could not be felt, neither at the radius nor at the temple bone, somnolency was general.

Often it happened that the moment they sank to the ground the lower extremities became paralyzed; soon after that, a few drops of blood from the nose indicated the moribund condition.

Severed were all bonds of brotherly love, extinguished all human feeling toward those who, from exhaustion, had fallen on the road.

Many men, among them his former best comrades and even relatives, would fall upon such an unfortunate one to divest him of his clothing and other belongings, to leave him naked on the snow, inevitably to die.

The impulse of self-preservation overmastered everything in them.

During the second half of November, and more so during the first days of December, especially on the 8th, 9th, and 10th, when the army arrived at Wilna, the cold had reached the lowest degree; during the night from December 9th to December 10th the thermometer showed -32 R (-40 F). The cold air caused severe pain in the eyes, resembling that of strong pressure. The eyes, weakened by the constant sight of snow, suffered greatly under these circumstances.

Many were blinded to such an extent that they could not see one step forward, could recognize nothing and had to find their way, like the blind in general, with the aid of a stick. Many of these fell during the march and became stiffened at once.

During this period von Scherer noticed that those who had been suffering very much from cold would die quickly when they had fallen to the frozen, ice-covered ground; the shaking due to the fall probably causing injury to the spinal cord, resulting in sudden general paralysis of the lower extremities, the bladder and the intestinal tract being affected to the extent of an involuntary voiding of urine and feces.

Surgeon-major von Keller stated to von Scherer the following case:

> I was lying near Wilna, it was during the first days of December, during one of the coldest nights, together with several German officers, on the road close to a camp fire, when a military servant approached us asking permission to bring his master, a French officer of the guards, to our fire.
>
> This permission was willingly granted, and two soldiers of the guard brought a tall and strong man of about thirty years of age whom they placed on the ground between themselves.
>
> When the Frenchman learned of the presence of a surgeon he narrated that something quite extraordinary had happened to him.
>
> Notwithstanding the great general misery, he had thus far been cheerful and well, but half an hour previous his feet had stiffened and he had been unable to walk, and now he had no longer any sensation from the toes up the legs.
>
> I examined him and found that his feet were completely stiff, white like marble, and ice cold.
>
> The officer was well dressed and, notwithstanding his pitiful condition, more cheerful than myself and my comrades.
>
> Soon he felt a strong desire to urinate, but was unable to do so.
>
> With great relish he ate a large piece of horse flesh which had been roasted at the fire, but soon complained of great illness.
>
> His cheerfulness changed suddenly to a sensation of great distress. Ischuria persisted for several hours and caused him great pain; later on during the night, he involuntarily voided feces and a large amount of urine. He slept a great deal, the breathing was free, but at dawn he fell into a helpless condition, and, at daybreak, before we had left the fire, this strong man, who eight to ten hours before had been in good health, died.

Most excellent and ingenious men in the prime of manhood all suffered more or less from the cold; with the exception of a few cases, the senses of all were, if not entirely deranged, at least weakened. The longest and sometimes complete resistance to the cold was offered by those who had always been of a cheerful disposition, especially those who had not become discouraged by the great privations and hardships, who ate horse flesh with relish and who in general had adapted themselves to circumstances.

One of the Wuerttembergian officers, a man of considerable military knowledge and experience, was attacked, a few days before reaching Wilna, with so pronounced a loss of sensation that he only vegetated, moving along in the column like a machine.

He had no bodily sickness, no fever, was fairly well in strength, had never or rarely been in want, but his whole sensory system was seriously affected by the cold.

Von Scherer saw him, after he arrived at an inn in Wilna, somewhat recovered by warmth and food, but acting childishly.

While he ate the food placed before him he would make terrible grimaces, crying or laughing for minutes at a time.

His constitution badly shaken, but gradually improving, he returned home, and it took a long time before he recovered completely.

All traces of his sickness disappeared finally, and as active as ever he attended his former duties.

Another officer, with whom von Scherer travelled a few days between Krasnoe and Orscha, had not until then suffered any real want.

He rode in a well-closed carriage drawn by strong horses, had two soldiers as servants, was well dressed and suffered, therefore, much less than others. Especially was he well protected from the cold, yet this had a severe effect on him. His mind became deranged, he did not recognize von Scherer with whom he had been on intimate terms for years, nor could he call either of his servants by name; he would constantly run alongside the carriage, insisting that it belonged to the French emperor and that he was entrusted to guard his majesty.

Only when he had fallen asleep, or by force, was von Scherer able, with the aid of the two servants, to place him in the carriage.

His mental condition became worse every day; von Scherer had to leave him.

This officer reached Wilna, where he was made a prisoner and soon died in captivity.

Many more cases resembling these two were observed by von Scherer, and other army surgeons reported instances of the like effect of cold.

Surgeon General von Schmetter had remained with the Crown Prince of Wuerttemberg in Wilna, while the army marched to Moscow.

He reported many cases of unfortunates whom he had received in the hospital in Wilna, who by cold and misery of all kinds had been reduced to a pitiful state—men formerly of a vigorous constitution presented a puerile appearance and had become demented.

A cavalryman of the regiment Duke Louis, who, during February, 1813, had been admitted into the hospital of Wilna, suffering from quiet mania without being feverish, was constantly searching for something.

Hands and feet had been frozen. He became ill with typhus and was more or less delirious for two weeks.

After the severity of the sickness had abated he again began to search anxiously for something, and after the fever had left him he explained that thirty thousand florins, which he had brought with him to the hospital, had been taken away.

It was learned that this cavalryman had been sent, together with other comrades, with dispatches to Murat; that these men had defended Murat with great bravery when he was in danger in the battle of Borodino.

Murat, in recognition of their bravery, which had saved him, had given them a wagon with gold, which they were to divide among themselves.

The share of each of these cavalrymen amounted to over thirty thousand florins, and the gold was transported on four horses, but these horses, for want of food, had broken down under the load, and the gold had fallen into the hands of the Cossacks.

The patient became quite ecstatic when, during his convalescence, he was told that he had brought no gold with him into the hospital; only gradually could he be made to understand that he had been mistaken.

He said, however, that he could not recollect having been robbed during the retreat, although this fact had been testified to by two witnesses.

Two years after he had left the hospital and quitted the military service, when he was perfectly well and vigorous again, he recollected that on a very cold day he had been taken prisoner by Cossacks, who had left him, naked and unconscious, in the snow.

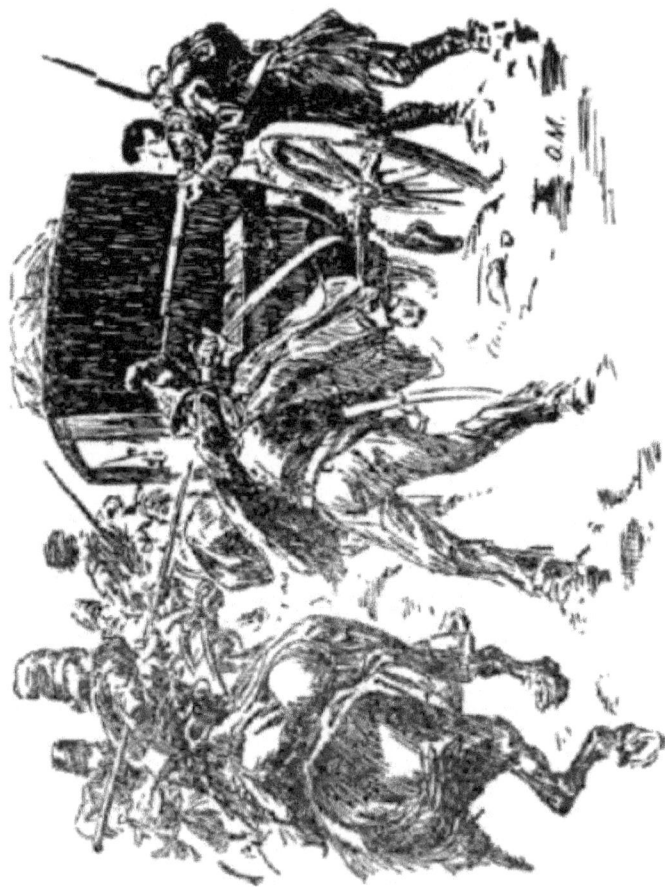

Attack of Cossacks

He could not remember how and when he had come into the hospital. Notwithstanding all these later recollections, he still imagined from time to time that he had brought the gold with him into the hospital.

Surgeon General von Schmetter reported further the case of a cavalryman of the King's regiment who, like many others, had returned from Russia in an imbecile condition.

He spoke alternately, or mixed up, Polish, Russian, and German; he had to be fed like a child, could not remember his name or the name of his native place, and died from exhaustion eight days after admittance into the hospital.

On necropsy of the quite wrinkled body, the cerebral vessels were found full of blood, the ventricles full of serum. On the surface of the brain between the latter and the meninges were found several larger and smaller sacs filled with lymph, the spinal canal full of serum; in the spinal cord plain traces of inflammation. In the lungs there was much dark coagulated blood, and likewise in the *vena cava;* in the stomach and intestines, many cicatrices; the mesenteric glands and pancreas were much degenerated and filled with pus; the rectum showed many cicatrices and several ulcers.

In the hospital of Mergentheim eight necropsies were held on corpses of soldiers who had returned mentally affected in consequence of exposure to extreme cold. Similar conditions had presented themselves in all these cases.

Surgeon General von Kohlreuter attended an infantry officer who had arrived at Inorawlow, in Poland, where the remainder of the Wuerttembergian corps had rallied. He showed no special sickness, had no fever, but fell into complete apathy. For a long time he had great weakness of mind, but recovered completely in the end.

Of another patient of this kind, an officer of the general staff, who had been treated after that fatal retreat from Moscow, von Kohlreuter reports that later on he recovered completely from the mental derangement, but died on his return, near the borders of Saxony, from exhaustion.

An infantry officer became mentally deranged sometime after he had returned to his home; it took a long time, but finally he recovered without special medical aid.

Recovery of such cases was accomplished by time, a mild climate, by social intercourse, and good nourishment; many of them, on the way through Germany and before they reached their own home, had completely regained their mental faculties, and only in a small number of cases did it take a long period of time and medication before recovery was assured.

The effect of intense cold on wounds was very severe: Violent inflammation, enormous swelling, gangrene—the latter often due to the impossibility of proper care. Larger wounds sometimes could not be dressed on the retreat, and while the cold weather lasted gangrene and death followed in quick succession. The effect of cold was noticed also on wounds which had healed and cicatrized.

Von Happrecht, an officer of the regiment Duke Louis, had been wounded in the foot by a cannon ball in the Battle of Borodino on September 7th, and Surgeon-General von Kohlreuter had amputated it. Fairly strong and cheerful, this officer arrived safely at the Beresina. The passage over this river was, as is well known, very dangerous, and von Happrecht had to wait, exposed to cold, for some time before he could cross. Soon after traversing on horseback he felt as if he had lost the stump; he had no sensation in the leg the foot of which had been amputated. Unfortunately, he approached a fire to warm himself and felt a severe pain in the stump; extensive inflammation, with swelling, set in; gangrene followed and, notwithstanding most skilful attendance, he died soon after his arrival at Wilna.

So far von Scherer. Beaupré, speaking of his own observations of the effects of extreme cold, gives the following account:

Soldiers unable to go further fell and resigned themselves to death, in that frightful state of despair which is caused by the total loss of moral and physical force, which was aggravated to the utmost by the sight of their comrades stretched lifeless on the snow. During a retreat so precipitate and fatal, in a country deprived of its resources, amid disorder and confusion, the sad physician was forced to remain an astonished spectator of evils he could not arrest, to which he could apply no remedy. The state of matters remarkably affected the moral powers. The consternation was general. Fear of not escaping the danger was very naturally allied with the desperate idea of seeing one's country no more. None could flatter himself that his courage and strength would suffice so that he would be able to withstand privations and sufferings beyond human endurance. Italians, Portuguese, Spaniards, those from the temperate and southern parts of France, obliged to brave an austere climate unknown to them, directed their thoughts toward their country and with good reasons regretted the beauty of the heaven, the softness of the air of the regions of their birth.

Nostalgia was common. . . . The army was but three days from Smolensk when the heavens became dark, and snow began to fall in great flakes, in such a quantity that the air was obscured. The cold was then felt with extreme severity; the northern wind blew impetuously into the faces of the soldiers and incommoded many who were no longer able to see. They strayed, fell into the snow—above all, when night surprised them—and thus miserably perished.

Disbanded regiments were reduced to almost nothing by the loss of men continually left behind either on the roads or in the bivouacs.

Of the days of Smolensk he writes:

In the streets one met with none but sick and wounded men asking for hospitals, soldiers of every sort, of every nation, going and coming, some of them trying to find a place where provisions were sold or distributed; others taciturn, incapable of any effort, absorbed by grief, half dead with cold, awaiting their last hour. On all sides there were complaints and groans, dead and dying soldiers, all of which presented a picture that was still further darkened by the ruinous aspect of the city.

At Smolensk Beaupré himself had a narrow escape from freezing to death; he narrates:

During the frightful night when we left Smolensk I felt much harassed; toward 5 in the morning, a feeling of lassitude impelled me to stop and rest. I sat down on the trunk of a birch, beside eight frozen corpses, and soon experienced an inclination to sleep, to which I yielded the more willingly as at that moment it seemed delicious. Fortunately I was aroused from that incipient somnolency—which infallibly would have brought on torpor—by the cries and oaths of two soldiers who were violently striking a poor exhausted horse that had fallen down.

I emerged from that state with a sort of shock.

The sight of what was beside me strongly recalled to my mind the danger to which I exposed myself; I took a little brandy and started to run to remove the numbness of my legs, the coldness and insensibility of which were as if they had been immersed in an iced bath.

He then describes his experience in similar cases:

It happened three or four times that I assisted some of those unfortunates who had just fallen and began to doze, to rise again and endeavoured to keep them in motion after having given them a little sweetened brandy.

It was in vain; they could neither advance nor support themselves, and they fell again in the same place, where of necessity they had to be abandoned to their unhappy lot. Their pulse was small and imperceptible. Respiration, infrequent and scarcely sensible in some, was attended in others by complaints and groans. Sometimes the eyes were open, fixed, dull, wild, and the brain was seized by a quiet delirium; in other instances the eyes were red and manifested a transient excitement of the brain; there was marked delirium in these cases. Some stammered incoherent words, others had a reserved and convulsive cough. In some blood flowed from the nose and ears; they agitated their limbs as if groping.

(This description of Beaupré complements the account given by von Scherer.)

Many had their hands, feet, and ears frozen. A great many were mortally stricken when obliged to stop to relieve nature; the arrival of that dreaded moment was in fact very embarrassing, on account of the danger of exposing oneself to the air as well as owing to the numbness of the fingers which rendered them unable to readjust the clothes. . . . And they travelled day and night, often without knowing where they were.

Ultimately they were obliged to stop, and, complaining, shivering, forced to lie down in the woods, on the roads, in ditches, at the bottom of ravines, often without fire, because they had no wood at hand, nor strength enough to go and cut some in the vicinity; if they succeeded in lighting one, they warmed themselves as they could, and fell asleep without delay.

The first hours of sleep were delightful, but, alas! they were merely the deceitful precursor of death that was waiting for them.

The fire at length became extinct for want of attention or owing to the great blast. Instead of finding safety in the sweets of sleep, they were seized and benumbed by cold, and never saw daylight again. . . .

I have seen them sad, pale, despairing, without arms, staggering, scarce able to sustain themselves, their heads hanging to the right or left, their extremities contracted, setting their feet on the coals, lying down on hot cinders, or falling into the fire,

"And never saw daylight again."

which they sought mechanically, as if by instinct.

Others apparently less feeble, and resolved not to allow themselves to be depressed by misfortune, rallied their powers to avoid sinking; but often they quitted one place only to perish in another.

Along the road, in the adjacent ditches and fields, were perceived human carcasses, heaped up and lying at random in fives, tens, fifteens and twenties, of such as had perished during the night, which was always more murderous than the day.

When no longer able to continue walking, having neither strength nor will power, they fell on their knees.

The muscles of the trunk were the last to lose the power of contraction.

Many of those unfortunates remained for some time in that posture contending with death.

Once fallen it was impossible for them, even with their utmost efforts, to rise again. The danger of stopping had been universally observed; but, alas! presence of mind and firm determination did not always suffice to ward off mortal attacks made from all directions upon one miserable life!

Wiasma

About a mile and a half from Wiasma the enemy appeared to the left of the road, and his fire happened to strike the midst of the tail of the army, composed of disbanded soldiers without arms, with wounded and sick among them, and women and children. Every artillery discharge of the Russians caused frightful cries and a frightful commotion in the helpless mass.

And the rear guard, in trying to make them advance, ill-treated them, the soldiers who had clung to the flag assumed the right to despise those who, either voluntarily or under compulsion, had abandoned it.

Of the old generals of Davout some had been killed, Friant was so severely wounded that he could not be about, Compans had been wounded in the arm, Moraud in the head, but these two, the former with one arm in a sling, the other with a bandaged head, were on horseback, surrounding the marshal commanding the first corps which had been reduced to 15 thousand from 20 thousand at Moshaisk, from 28 thousand in Moscow, and from 72 thousand crossing the Niemen. The remaining 15 thousand were all old warriors whose iron constitution had triumphed.

The Battle of Wiasma took place on the 2nd of November. The Russians under Miloradovitch had 100 cannon, whereas the French under Ney, Davout, and the wounded generals named above, had only forty. This day cost the French 1,500 to 1,800 men in killed and wounded, and, as mentioned, these were of the oldest and best; the loss of the Russians was twice that number, but their wounded were not lost, while it was impossible to save a single one of the French, for the latter had no attendance at all; the cold being very severe it killed them, and those who did not perish by the frost were put to death by the cruel, ferocious Russian peasants.

Entering Wiasma at night, nothing in the way of provisions was found; the guard and the corps which had been there before the battle had devoured everything. No provisions were left of those taken along from Moscow. The army passed a sombre and bitter cold night in a forest; great fires were lighted, horse meat was roasted, and the soldiers of Prince Eugene and of Marshal Davout, especially the latter who had been on their feet for three days, slept profoundly around great camp-fires. During two weeks they had been on duty to cover the retreat and during this time had lost more than one half of their number.

Napoleon arrived at Dorogobouge on November 5th, the Prince Eugene on the 6th, the other corps on the 7th and 8th.

Until then the frost had been severe but not yet fatal. All of a sudden, on the 9th, the weather changed, and there was a terrible snowstorm.

On their way to Moscow the regiments had traversed Poland during a suffocating heat and had left their warm clothing in the magazines.

Some soldiers had taken furs with them from Moscow, but had sold them to their officers.

Well nourished, they could have stood the frost, but living on a little flour diluted with water, on horse meat roasted at the camp fire, sleeping on the ground without shelter, they suffered frightfully. We shall later on speak more in detail of the miserable clothing.

The first snow which had been falling after they had left Dorogobouge had seriously increased the general misery. Except among the soldiers of the rear guard which had been commanded with inflexible firmness by Davout, and which was now led by Ney, the sense of duty began to be lost by almost all soldiers.

As we have learned, all the wounded had to be left to their fate, and soldiers who had been charged to escort Russian prisoners relieved themselves of their charge by shooting these prisoners dead.

The horses had not been shod in Russian fashion for travelling on the ice. The army had come during the summer without any idea of returning during the winter; the horses slipped on the ice, those of the artillery were too feeble to draw cannon even of small calibre, they were beaten unmercifully until they perished; not only cannons and ammunition had to be left, but the number of vehicles carrying necessities of life diminished from day to day. The soldiers lived on the fallen horses; when night came the dead animals were cut to pieces by means of the sabre, huge portions were roasted at immense fires, the men devoured them and went to sleep around the fires. If the Cossacks did not disturb their dearly bought sleep the men would awake; some half burnt, others finding themselves lying in the mud which had formed around them, and many would not rise any more. General von Kerner, of the Wuerttembergian troops had slept in a barn during the night from November 7th to November 8th. Coming out at daybreak he saw his men in the plain as they had lain down around a fire the evening before, frozen and dead. The survivors would depart, hardly glancing at the unfortunates who had died or were dying, and for whom they could do nothing.

The snow would soon cover them, and small eminences marked the places where these brave soldiers had been sacrificed for a foolish enterprise.

It was under these circumstances that Ney, the man of the greatest energy and of a courage which could not be shaken by any kind of suffering, took command of the rear guard, relieving Davout whose inflexible firmness and sense of honour and duty were not less admirable than the excellent qualities of Ney. The bravest of the brave, as Napoleon had called Ney, had an iron constitution, he never seemed to be tired nor suffering from any ailment; he passed the night without shelter, slept or did not sleep, ate or did not eat, without ever being discouraged; most of the time he was on his feet in the midst of his soldiers; he did not find it beneath the dignity of a Marshal of France, when necessary, to gather 50 or 100 men about him and lead them, like a simple captain of infantry, against the enemy under fire of musketry, calm, serene, believing himself invulnerable and being apparently so indeed; he did not find it incompatible with his rank to take up the musket of a soldier who had fallen and to fire at the enemy like a private. There is a great painting in the gallery of Versailles representing him in such an action. He had never been wounded in battle. And this great hero was executed in the morning of December 7th, 1815, in the garden of the Luxembourg.

Louis XVIII, this miserable and insignificant man of legitimate royal blood who had never rendered any service to France, wanted revenge—Ney was arrested and condemned by the Chamber of Peers after the marshals had refused to condemn him. His wife pleaded in vain for his life, the king remained inflexible. Ney was simply shot by twelve poor soldiers commanded for the execution. After the marshal had sunk down, an Englishman suddenly rode up at a gallop and leaped over the fallen hero, to express the triumph of the victors. It was in as bad taste as everything that England contrived against Napoleon and his men.[1]

Among the spectators there was also a Russian general in full uniform and on horseback. Tzar Alexander expelled him from the army after he had heard of it.

The Bourbons commenced a tromocraty which was called, in contrast to the terrorisms of the revolution, the white terror.

Much has been written about the fantastic costume of Murat, but I do not recollect having read the true explanation of it. All writers agree that he was the bravest, the greatest cavalry general. As such he meant to be distinguished from far and near in the midst of the battle where danger was greatest, so that the sight of his person, his exposure to the enemy, should encourage and inspire his soldiers. He rode a very noble white horse and wore a Polish *kurtka* of light blue velvet which reached down to the knees, embroidered with golden lace, dark red mameluke pantaloons with golden galloons, white gauntlets and a three-cornered general's hat with white plumes; the saddle was of red velvet and a caparison of the same stuff, all embroidered with gold. The neck of the king was bare, a large white scalloped collar fell over the collar of the *kurtka*. A strong black full beard gave a martial expression to his face with the fiery eyes and regular features. Sometimes he wore a *biretta* with a diamond agraffe and a high plume of heron feathers. Very seldom he appeared in the uniform of a marshal.

And this other great hero, who, like Ney, had never been wounded in battle, was executed by order of the court of Naples on October 13th, 1815, in the hall of Castle Pizzo.

---

1. Brave men were condemned to deportation or were executed; derision and mocking of Napoleon's generals was the order of the day.

Vop

In order to give an idea of the great difficulties the soldiers had to face, and examples of their heroic behaviour under trying circumstances, let us relate the disaster of Vop.

While Napoleon, with the imperial guard, the corps of Marshal Davout and a mass of stragglers, all escorted by Marshal Ney, was marching on the road to Smolensk, Prince Eugene had taken the road to Doukhowtchina. The prince had with him six or seven thousand men under arms, including the Italian guard, some Bavarian cavalry which still had their horses and their artillery mounted, and also many stragglers, with these a number of families who had been following the Italian division.

At the end of the first day's journey—it was on November 8th—near the castle Zazale, they hoped to find at this castle some provisions and an abode for the night. A great cold had set in, and when they came to a hill the road was so slippery that it was almost impossible to negotiate the elevation with even the lightest load. Detaching horses from the pieces in order to double and treble the teams they succeeded in scaling the height with cannons of small calibre, but they were forced to abandon the larger ones.

The men being exhausted as well as the horses they felt humiliated at being obliged to leave their best pieces. While they had exerted themselves with such sad results, Platow had followed them with his Cossacks and light cannons mounted on sleighs and incessantly fired into the French. The commander of the Italian artillery, General Anthouard, was severely wounded and was compelled to give up his command.

A gloomy night was passed at the castle Zazale.

On the morning of the 9th they left at an early hour to cross the Vop, a little rivulet during the summer but now quite a river, at least four feet deep and full of mud and ice.

The pontooneers of Prince Eugene had gone ahead, working during the night to construct a bridge, but frozen and hungry they had suspended their work for a few hours, to finish it after a short rest.

At daybreak those most anxious to cross went on the unfinished bridge which they thought was completed.

A heavy mist prevented them from recognizing their error until the first ones fell into the icy water emitting piercing cries. Finally horses and men waded through the water—some succeeded, other succumbed.

It would lead too far to give here a full description of the distressing scenes, the difficulty of passing with artillery and the mostly vain attempts to bring over the baggage wagons. But, to cap the climax, there arrived three or four thousand Cossacks shouting savagely. With the greatest difficulty only was the rear guard able to keep them at a distance so that they could not come near enough to make use of their lances. Their artillery, however, caused veritable desolation.

Among the poor fugitives from Moscow there were a number of Italian and French women; these unfortunates stood at the border of the river, crying and embracing their children, but not daring to wade through it. Brave soldiers, full of humanity, took the little ones in their arms and passed with them, some repeating this two and three times, in order to bring all the children safely over. These desolate families, not being able to save their vehicles, lost with them the means of subsistence brought from Moscow. All the baggage, the entire artillery with the exception of seven or eight pieces, had been lost, and a thousand men had been killed by the fire of the Cossacks.

This dreadful event on the retreat from Moscow is called the disaster of Vop and was the precursor of another disaster of the same nature, but a hundred times more frightful, the disaster of the Beresina.

★★★★★★

There was another cause of death of which we have not spoken yet: this was the action of the heat at the campfires. Anxious to warm themselves, most of the soldiers hastened to bring their limbs near the flame; but this sudden exposure to extreme heat, after having suffered from the other extreme—cold—was acting on the feeble circulation in the tissues and produced gangrene of the feet, the hands, even of the face, causing paralysis either partial, of the extremities, or general, of the whole body.

Only those were saved who had been able to keep up their circulation by means of hot drinks or other stimulants and who, noticing numbness, had rubbed the affected parts with snow. Those who did not or could not resort to these precautions found themselves paralyzed, or stricken with sudden gangrene, in the morning when the camp broke up.

The hospitals of Koenigsberg admitted about ten thousand soldiers of Napoleon's army, only a small number of whom had been wounded, most of them with frozen extremities, who had, as the physicians of that time called it, a pest, the fever of congelation which was terribly contagious.

The heroic Larrey although exhausted from fatigue had come to these hospitals to take care of the sick, but he became infected with the contagion himself and was taken sick.

A great calamity was the want of shoes; we have seen that this was already felt in Moscow, before they set out on the endless march over ice and snow.

The soldiers had their feet wrapped in rags, pieces of felt or leather, and when a man had fallen on the road some of his comrades would cut off his feet and carry them to the next camp fire to remove the rags—for their own use.

But the general appearance of the emaciated soldiers with long beards, and faces blackened by the smoke of camp-fires, the body wrapped in dirty rags of wearing apparel brought from Moscow, was such that it was difficult to recognize them as soldiers.

And the vermin! Carpon, a surgeon-major of the grand army, in describing the days of Wilna which were almost as frightful as the disaster of the Beresina, speaks on this subject. It is revolting. Strange to say, it is hardly ever mentioned in the medical history of wars, although everyone who has been in the field is quite familiar with it.

At last I have found—in Holzhausen's book—a description of the most revolting lice plague (phtheiriasis) from which, according to his valet, Constant, even the emperor was not exempted. As a matter of course under the circumstances—impossibility of bodily cleanliness— this vermin developed in a way which baffles description. Suckow, a Wuerttembergian first lieutenant, speaks of it as causing intolerable distress, disturbing the sleep at the campfire. Johann von Borcke became alarmed when he discovered that his whole body was eaten up by these insects. A French colonel relates that in scratching himself he tore a piece of flesh from the neck, but that the pain caused by this wound produced a sensation of relief.

Smolensk

All the corps marched to Smolensk where they expected to reach the end of all their misery and to find repose, food, shelter; in fact, all they were longing for.

Napoleon entered the city with his guards and kept the rest of the army, including the stragglers, out of doors until arrangements could have been made for the regular distribution of rations and quarters. But together with the stragglers the mass of the army became unmanageable and resorted to violence.

Seeing that the guards were given the preference they broke out in revolt, entered by force and pillaged the magazines. "The magazines are pillaged!" was the general cry of terror and despair. Everyone was running to grasp something to eat.

Finally, something like order was established to save some of the provisions for the corps of Prince Eugene and Marshal Ney who arrived after fighting constantly to protect the city from the troops of the enemy. They received in their turn eatables and a little rest, not under shelter but in the streets, where they were protected, not from the frost, but from the enemy.

There were no longer any illusions. The army having hoped to find shelter and protection, subsistence, clothes and, above all, shoes, at Smolensk, they found nothing of all this and learned that they had to leave, perhaps the next day, to recommence the interminable march without abode for the night, without bread to eat and constantly righting while exhausted, with the cruel certainty that if wounded they would be the prey of wolves and vultures.

This prospect made them all desperate; they saw the abyss, and still the worst was yet in store for them: Beresina and Wilna!

Napoleon left Smolensk on November 14th. The cold had become more intense—21 deg. Reaumur (16 deg. below zero Fahrenheit)—

this is the observation of Larrey who had a thermometer attached to his coat; he was the only one who kept a record of the temperature.

The cold killed a great many, and the road became covered with dead soldiers resting under the snow.

To the eternal honour of the most glorious of all armies be it said that it was only at the time when the misery had surpassed all boundaries, when the soldiers had to camp on the icy ground with an empty stomach, their limbs paralyzed in mortal rigor, that the dissolution began.

It was even after the heroic Battle of Wiasma that they fought day for day.

It was not the cold which caused the proud army to disband, but hunger.

Provisions could nowhere be found; all horses perished, and with them the possibility of transporting food and ammunition.

And it is one thing to suffer cold and hunger, travelling under ordinary circumstances, and another to suffer thus and at the same time being followed by the enemy.

Beresina

In order to understand the disaster of the Beresina it is necessary to cast a glance at the condition of Napoleon's army at that time.

After the battle at Krasnoe, Napoleon at Orscha, on November 19th, happy to have found a place of safety at last, with well furnished magazines, made a new attempt to rally the army by means of a regular distribution of rations. A detachment of excellent gendarmes had come from France and was employed to do police duty, to engage everybody, either by persuasion or by force, to join his corps. These brave men, accustomed to suppress disorder in the rear of the army, had never witnessed anything like the condition with which they were obliged to deal at this time. They were dismayed. All their efforts were in vain. Threats, promises of rations if the soldiers would fall in line, were of no avail whatever.

The men, whether armed or not, thought it more convenient, above all more safe, to care for themselves instead of again taking up the yoke of honour, thereby taking the risk of being killed, or wounded,—which amounted to the same thing—they would not think of sacrificing their individual self for the sake of the whole. Some of the disbanded soldiers had retained their arms, but only to defend themselves against the Cossacks and to be better able to maraud. They lived from pillaging, taking advantage of the escort of the army, without rendering any service.

In order to warm themselves they would put fire to houses occupied by wounded soldiers, many of whom perished in the flames in consequence. They had become real ferocious beasts. Among these marauders were only very few old soldiers, for most of the veterans remained with the flag until death.

Napoleon addressed the guards, appealing to their sense of duty, saying that they were the last to uphold military honour, that they, above

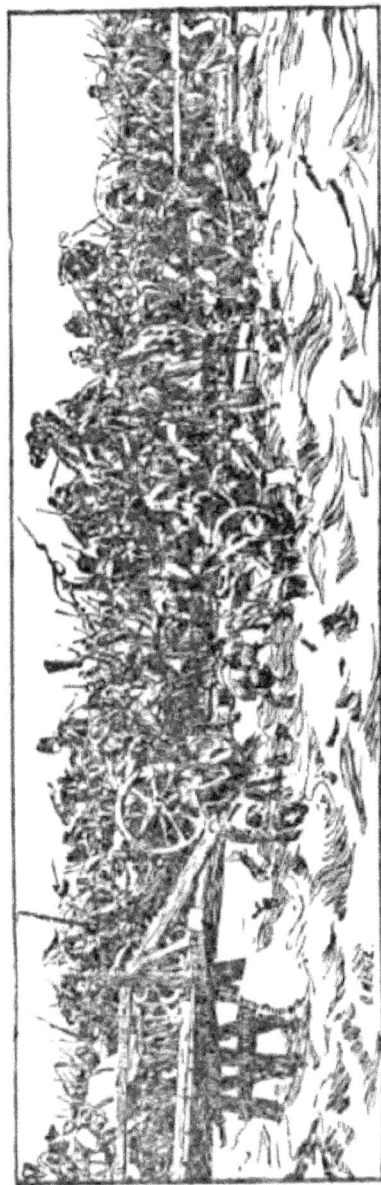

BERESINA

all, had to set the example to save the remainder of the army which was in danger of complete dissolution; that if they, the guards, would become guilty, they would be more guilty than any of the other corps, because they had no excuse to complain of neglect, for what few supplies had been at the disposal of the army, their wants had always been considered ahead of the rest of the army, that he could resort to punishments, could have shot the first of the old grenadiers who would leave the ranks, but that he preferred to rely on their virtue as warriors to assure their devotedness. The grenadiers expressed their assent and gave promises of good conduct. All surviving old grenadiers remained in the ranks, not one of them had disbanded. Of the six thousand who had crossed the Niemen, about 3,500 survived, the others had succumbed to fatigue or frost, very few had fallen in battle.

The disbanded soldiers of the rest of the army, having in view another long march, with great sufferings to endure, were not disposed to change their ways. They now needed a long rest, safety, and abundance, to make them recognize military discipline again. The order to distribute rations among those who had rallied around the flag could not be kept up for more than a few hours. The magazines were pillaged, as they had been pillaged at Smolensk. The forty-eight hours' stay at Orscha was utilized for rest and to nourish a few men and the horses.

In these days Napoleon was as indefatigable as he ever had been as young Bonaparte. His proclamation of the 19th did not remain quite unheeded even among the disbanded, but, on the march again, the nearer they came to the Beresina the more pronounced became the lack of discipline. In the following description I avail myself of the classical work of Thiers' *Histoire du Consulat et de l'Empire*.

The only bridge over the Beresina, at Borisow, had been burned by the Russians. It was as by miracle that General Corbineau met a Polish peasant who indicated a place—near the village Studianka—where the Beresina could be forded by horses. Napoleon, informed of this fact on November 28th, at once ordered General Eblé to construct the bridge and on November 25th, at 1 o'clock in the morning, he issued orders to Oudinot to have his corps ready for crossing the river. The moment had arrived when the great engineer, the venerable General Eblé, was to crown his career by an immortal service.

He had saved six cases containing tools, nails, clamps, and all kinds of iron pieces needed for the construction of trestle bridges. In his profound foresight he had also taken along two wagon-loads of charcoal, and he had under his command 400 excellent pontooneers upon whom he could reply absolutely.

General Eblé has been described as the model of an officer, on account of his imposing figure and his character.

Eblé and Larrey were the two men whom the whole army never ceased to respect and to obey, even when they demanded things which were almost impossible. General Eblé then with his 400 men departed in the evening of November 24th for Borisow, followed by the clever General Chasseloup who had some sappers with him, but without their tools. General Chasseloup was a worthy associate of the illustrious chief of the pontooneers. They marched all night, arriving at Borisow on the 25th, at 5 o'clock in the morning. There they left some soldiers in order to deceive the Russians by making them believe that the bridge was to be constructed below Borisow. Eblé with his pontooneers, however, marched through swamps and woods along the river as far as Studianka, arriving there during the afternoon of the 25th.

Napoleon in his impatience wanted the bridges finished on that day, an absolute impossibility; it could not be done until the 26th, by working all night, and not to rest until this was accomplished was . the firm resolution of these men who by that time had marched two days and two nights. General Eblé spoke to his pontooneers, telling them that the fate of the army was in their hands. He inspired them with noble sentiments and received the promise of the most absolute devotedness. They had to work in the bitter cold weather—severe frost having suddenly set in—all night and during the next day, in the water, in the midst of floating ice, probably under fire of the enemy, without rest, almost without time to swallow some boiled meat; they had not even bread or salt or brandy. This was the price at which the army could be saved. Each and every one of the pontooneers pledged himself to their general, and we shall see how they kept their word.

Not having time to fell trees and to cut them into planks, they demolished the houses of the unfortunate village Studianka and took all the wood which could serve for the construction of bridges; they forged the iron needed to fasten the planks and in this way they made the trestles. At daybreak of the 26th they plunged these trestles into the Beresina. Napoleon, together with some of his generals, Murat, Berthier, Eugene, Caulaincourt, Duroc, and others, had hastened to Studianka on this morning to witness the progress of Eblé's work. Their faces expressed the greatest anxiety, for at this moment the question was whether or not the master of the world would be taken prisoner by the Russians. He watched the men working, exerting all their might in strength and intelligence.

But it was by no means sufficient to plunge bravely into the icy water and to fasten the trestles, the almost superhuman work had to be accomplished in spite of the enemy whose outposts were visible on the other side of the river. Were there merely some Cossacks, or was there a whole army corps? This was an important question to solve. One of the officers, Jacqueminot, who was as brave as he was intelligent, rode into the water, traversed the Beresina, the horse swimming part of the way, and reached the other shore. On account of the ice the landing was very difficult.

In a little wood he found some Cossacks, but altogether only very few enemies could be seen. Jacqueminot then turned back to bring the good news to the emperor. As it was of the greatest importance to secure a prisoner to obtain exact information about what was to be feared or to be hoped, the brave Jacqueminot once more crossed the Beresina, this time accompanied by some determined cavalry men. They overpowered a Russian outpost, the men sitting around a fire, took a corporal with them, and brought this prisoner before Napoleon who learned to his great satisfaction that Tchitchakoff with his main force was before Borisow to prevent the passage of the French, and that at Studianka there was only a small detachment of light troops.

It was necessary to take advantage of these fortunate circumstances. But the bridges were not ready. The brave General Corbineau with his cavalry brigade crossed the river under the above-described difficulties, and established himself in the woods. Napoleon mounted a battery of forty cannons on the left shore, and now the French could flatter themselves to be masters of the right shore while the bridges were made, and that their whole army would be able to cross. Napoleon's star seemed to brighten again, the officers grouped around him, saluting with expressions of joy, such as they had not shown for a long time.

All was now depending on the completion of the bridges, for there were two to be constructed, each 600 feet in length; one on the left for wagons, the other, on the right, for infantry and cavalry. A hundred pontooneers had gone into the water and with the aid of little floats built for this purpose, had commenced the fixation of the trestles. The water was freezing and formed ice crusts around their shoulders, arms, and legs, ice crusts which adhered to the flesh and caused great pain. They suffered without complaining, without appearing to be affected, so great was their ardour. The river at that point was 300 feet wide and with twenty-three trestles for each bridge the two shores could be united. In order to transport first the troops, all efforts were concentrated on the construction of the bridge to the right—that is, the one for infantry and cavalry—and at 1 o'clock in the afternoon it was ready.

About nine thousand men of the corps of Marshal Oudinot passed over the first bridge and under great precautions took two cannons along. Arrived on the other side, Oudinot faced some troops of infantry which General Tschaplitz, the commander of the advance guard of Tchitchakoff, had brought there. The engagement was very lively but of short duration. The French killed 200 men of the enemy and were able to establish themselves in a good position, from where they could cover the passage. Time was given now for the passage of enough troops to meet Tchitchakoff, during the rest of the day, the 26th and the succeeding night. Concerning many details I have to refer to Thiers' description.

At 4 o'clock in the afternoon the second bridge was completed. Napoleon, on the Studianka side, yet supervised everything; he wanted to remain among the last to cross the bridge. General Eblé, without himself taking a moment of rest, had one-half the number of his pontooneers rest on straw while the other half took up the painful task of guarding the bridges, of doing police duty, and of making repairs in case of accidents, until they were relieved by the others. On this day the infantry guards and what remained of cavalry guards marched over the bridge, followed by the artillery train.

Unfortunately, the left bridge, intended for vehicles, shook too much under the enormous weight of wagons following one another without interruption. Pressed as they were, the pontooneers had not had time to shape the timber forming the path, they had to use wood as they found it, and in order to deaden the rumbling of the wagons they had put moss, hemp, straw—in fact, everything they could gather in Studianka—into the crevices. But the horses removed this kind of litter with their feet, rendering the surface of the path very rough, so that it had formed undulations, and at 8 o'clock in the evening three trestles gave way and fell, together with the wagons which they carried, into the Beresina. The heroic pontooneers went to work again, going into the water which was so cold that ice immediately formed anew where it had been broken. With their axes they had to cut holes into the ice to place new trestles six, seven and even eight feet deep into the river were the bridge had given way. At 11 o'clock the bridge was secure again.

General Eblé, who had always one relief at work while the other was asleep, took no rest himself. He had extra trestles made in case of another accident. At 2 o'clock in the morning three trestles of the left bridge, that is the one for the vehicles, gave way, unfortunately in the middle of the current, where the water had a depth of seven or eight feet. This time the pontooneers had to accomplish their difficult task in the darkness. The men, shaking from cold and starving, could not work anymore. The venerable General Eblé, who was not young as they were and had not taken rest as they had, suffered more than they did, but he had the moral superiority and spoke to them, appealing to their devotedness, told them of the certain disaster which would annihilate the whole army if they did not repair the bridges; and his address made a deep impression. With supreme self-denial they went to work again. General Lauriston, who had been sent by the emperor to learn the cause of the new accident, pressed Eblé's hand and, shedding tears, said to him: "For God's sake, hasten!"

Without showing impatience, Eblé, who generally had the roughness of a strong and proud soul, answered with kindness: "You see what we are doing," and he turned to his men to encourage, to direct them, and notwithstanding his age—he was 54 years old—he plunged into that icy water, which those young men were hardly able to endure (and this fact is stated by all the historians whose works I have read). At 6 o'clock in the morning (November 27th) this second accident had been repaired, the artillery train could pass again.

The bridge to the right—for infantry—did not have to endure the same kind of shaking up as the other bridge, and did not for one moment get out of order. If the stragglers and fugitives had obeyed all could have crossed during the night from November 26th to November 27th. But the attraction of some barns, some straw to lie on, some eatables found at Studianka, had retained a good many on this side of the river. The swamps surrounding the Beresina were frozen, which was a great advantage, enabling the people to walk over them. On these frozen swamps had been lighted thousands of fires, and ten thousand or fifteen thousand individuals had established themselves around them and did not want to leave. Soon they should bitterly regret the loss of a precious opportunity.

In the morning, on November 27th, Napoleon crossed the Beresina, together with all who were attached to his headquarters, and selected for his new headquarters the little village Zawnicky, on the other side of the Beresina. In front of him was the corps of Oudinot. All day long he was on horseback personally to hasten the passage of detachments of the army, somewhat over five thousand men under arms. Toward the end of the day the first corps arrived, under Davout, who since Krasnoe had again commanded the rear guard. This was the only corps which still had some military appearance.

The day of November 27th was occupied to cross the Beresina and to prepare for a desperate resistance, for the Russians could no longer be deceived as to the location of the bridges. At 2 o'clock in the afternoon a third accident happened, again on the bridge to the left. It was soon repaired, but the vehicles arrived in great numbers, and all were pressing forward in such a way that the gendarmes had extraordinary difficulties to enforce some order.

The 9th corps, that of Marshal Victor, had taken a position between Borisow and Studianka, in order to protect the army at the latter place. It had been foreseen that the crossing would be little interfered with during the first two days, the 26th and 27th, because Tchitchakoff was as yet ignorant of the real points elected for the bridges, expecting to find the French army below Borisow on the other side of the Beresina. Wittgenstein and Kutusoff had not yet had time to unite and did not sufficiently press the French.

Napoleon had good reasons to expect that the 28th would be the decisive day. He was resolved to save the army or to perish with it. Taking the greatest pains to deceive Tchitchakoff as long as possible he ordered Marchal Victor to leave the division Partouneaux, which had been reduced by marches and fights from 12 thousand to 4 thousand combatants, at Borisow. Victor with nine thousand men and 700 to 800 horses was to cover Studianka.

These nine thousand were the survivors of twenty-four thousand with whom Victor had left Smolensk to join Oudinot on the Oula. During one month's marching and in various engagements ten thousand to eleven thousand had been lost. The bearing, however, of those who survived was excellent, and seeing what was left of the grand army, the glory of which had, not long ago, been the object of their jealousy, in its present condition, they were stricken with pity and asked their oppressed comrades who had almost lost their pride as a result of the misery, what calamity could have befallen them? "You will soon be the same as we are," sadly answered the victors of Smolensk and Borodino.

The hour of the supreme crisis had come. The enemy, having now learned the truth, came to attack the French when many of them had not yet crossed the Beresina and were divided between the two sides of the river. Wittgenstein, who with three thousand men had followed the corps of Victor, was behind the latter between Borisow and Studianka, and ready with all his might to throw Victor into the Beresina. Altogether, including the forces of Tchitchakoff, there were about seventy-two thousand Russians, without counting thirty thousand men of Kutusoff in the rear, ready to fall on Victor's twelve thousand to thirteen thousand and Oudinot's seven thousand or eight thousand of the guards; twenty-eight thousand to thirty thousand French were divided between the two shores of the Beresina hampered by forty thousand stragglers, to fight, during the difficult operation of crossing the Beresina, with seventy-two thousand partly in front, partly in the rear.

This terrible struggle began in the evening of the 27th. The unfortunate French division of Partouneaux, the best of the three of Victor's corps, had received orders from Napoleon to remain before Borisow during the 27th, in order to deceive, as long as possible, and to detain Tchitchakoff. In this position Partouneaux was separated from his corps which, as we have seen, was concentrated around Studianka, by three miles of wood and swamps. As could be easily foreseen, Partouneaux was cut off by the arrival of the troops of Platow, Miloradovitch, and Yermaloff, who had followed the French on the road from Orscha to Borisow. In the evening of the 27th Partouneaux recognized his desperate position. With the immense dangers threatening him were combined the hideous embarrassment of several thousand stragglers who, believing in the passage below Borisow, had massed at that point, with their baggage, awaiting the construction of the bridge. The better to deceive the enemy they had been left in their error, and now they were destined to be sacrificed, together with the division of Partouneaux, on account of the terrible necessity to deceive Tchitchakoff.

When the bullets came from all sides, the confusion soon reached the climax; the three little brigades of Partouneaux forming for defence found themselves entangled with several thousand stragglers and fugitives who clamorously threw themselves into their ranks; the women of the mass, with baggage, especially with their frightful, piercing cries, characterized this scene of desolation. General Partouneaux decided to extricate himself, to open a way or to perish. He was with a thousand men against forty thousand. Several challenges to surrender he refused, and kept on fighting. The enemy, likewise exhausted, suspended firing toward midnight, being certain to take the last of this handful of braves who resisted so heroically in the morning. With daybreak the Russian generals again challenged General Partouneaux, who was standing upright in the snow with the 400 or 500 of his brigade, remonstrating with him, and he, with desperation in his soul, surrendered. The other two brigades of his division that had been separated from him also laid down their arms. The Russians took about two thousand prisoners, that is, the survivors of Partouneaux's division of four thousand, only one battalion of 300 men had succeeded, during the darkness of the night, in making its escape and reaching Studianka.

The army at Studianka had heard, during this cruel night, the sound of the cannonade and fusillade from the direction of Borisow. Napoleon and Victor were in great anxiety; the latter thought that the measure taken, *i.e.*, the sacrifice of his best division, of four thousand men who would have been of great value, had been unjustifiable, because after the crossing had begun on the 26th it was no longer possible to deceive the enemy.

The night was passed in cruel suspense, but being the prey of sorrows of so many kinds the French could hardly pay due attention to the many new ones which presented themselves at every moment. The silence which reigned on the morning of the 28th indicated the catastrophe of the division Partouneaux.

The firing now began on the two sides of the Beresina, on the right shore against the troops that had crossed, on the left against those covering the passage of the rear of the army. From this moment on nothing was thought of but fight. The cannonade and fusillade soon became extremely violent, and Napoleon, on horseback, incessantly riding from one point to another, assumed that Oudinot resisted Tchitchakoff while Eblé continued to care for the bridges, and that Victor, who was fighting Wittgenstein, was not thrown into the icy floods of the Beresina together with the masses which had not yet crossed.

Although the firing was terrible on all sides and thousands were killed on this lugubrious field; the French resisted on both banks of the river.

For the description of this battle I desire to refer to Thiers' great work. Taking all circumstances into consideration, it did the greatest honour to Napoleon's guns, to the valour of his generals and of his soldiers.

The confusion was frightful among the masses that had neglected to cross in time, and those who had arrived too late for the opportunity. Many, ignoring that the first bridge was reserved for pedestrians and horsemen, the second for wagons, crowded with delirious impatience upon the second bridge. The pontooneers on guard at the entrance of the bridge to the right were ordering the vehicles to the one on the left, which was 600 feet farther down. This precaution was an absolute necessity, because the bridge to the right could not endure the weight of the wagons. Those who were directed by the pontooneers to go to the other bridge had the greatest difficulty to pass through the compact masses pressing and pushing to enter the structure. A terrible struggle!

Opposing currents of people paralyzed all progress. The bullets of the enemy, striking into this dense crowd, produced fearful furrows and cries of terror from the fugitives; women with children, many on wagons, added to the horror. All pressed, all pushed; the stronger ones trampled on those who had lost their foothold, and killed many of the latter. Men on horseback were crushed, together with their horses, many of the animals becoming unmanageable, shot forward, kicked, reared, turned into the crowd and gained a little space by throwing people down into the river; but soon the space filled up again, and the mass of people was as dense as before.

This pressing forward and backward, the cries, the bullets striking into the helpless crowd, presented an atrocious scene—the climax of that forever odious and senseless expedition of Napoleon.

The excellent General Eblé, whose heart broke at this spectacle, tried in vain to establish a little order. Placing himself at the head of the bridge he addressed the multitude; but it was only by means of the bayonet that at last some improvement was brought about, and some women, children, and wounded were saved.

Some historians have stated that the French themselves fired cannon shots into the crowd, but this is not mentioned by Thiers. This panic was the cause that more than half the number of those perished who otherwise could have crossed. Many threw themselves, or were pushed, into the water and drowned. And this terrible conflict among the masses having lasted all day, far from diminishing, it became more horrible with the progress of the battle between Victor and Wittgenstein. The description of this battle I omit, referring again to Thiers, confining myself to give some figures.

Of 700 to 800 men of General Fournier's cavalry hardly 300 survived; of Marshal Victor's infantry, hardly five thousand. Of all these brave men, mostly Dutchmen, Germans, and Polanders, who had been sacrificed there was quite a number of wounded who might have been saved, but who had perished for want of all means of transportation. The Russians lost ten thousand to eleven thousand.

This double battle on the two shores of the Beresina is one of the most glorious in the history of France; 28 thousand against 72 thousand Russians. These 28 thousand could have been taken or annihilated to the last man, and it was almost a miracle that even a part of the army escaped this disaster.

With nightfall some calm came over this place of carnage and confusion.

On the next morning Napoleon had to recommence, this time not to retreat, but to flee; he had to wrest from the enemy the five thousand men of Marshal Victor's corps, Victor's artillery and as many as possible of those unfortunates who had not employed the two days by crossing. Napoleon ordered Marshal Victor to cross during the night with his corps and with all his artillery, and to take with him as many as possible of the disbanded and of the refugees who were still on that other side of the river.

Here we now learn of a singular flux and reflux of the frightened masses. While the cannon had roared, everyone wanted to cross but could not, now when with nightfall the firing had ceased they did not think any more of the danger of hesitation, not of the cruel lesson which they had learned during the day. They only wanted to keep away from the scene of horror which the crossing of the bridge had presented. It was a great task to force these unfortunates to cross the bridges before they were set on fire, a measure which was an absolute necessity and which was to be executed on the next morning.

The first work for Eblé's pontooneers was now to clear the avenues of the bridges from the mass of the dead, men and horses, of demolished wagons, and of all sorts of impediments. This task could be accomplished only in part; the mass of cadavers was too great for the time given for the removal of all of them, and those who crossed had to walk over flesh and blood.

In the night, from 9 o'clock to midnight, Marshal Victor crossed the Beresina, thereby exposing himself to the enemy, who, however, was too tired to think of fighting. He brought his artillery over the left bridge, his infantry over the right one, and with the exception of the wounded and two pieces of artillery, all his men and all his material safely reached the other side. The crossing accomplished, he erected a battery to hold the Russians in check and to prevent them from crossing the bridges.

There remained several thousand stragglers and fugitives on this side of the Beresina who could have crossed during the night but had refused to do so. Napoleon had given orders to destroy the bridges at daybreak and had sent word to General Eblé and Marshal Victor to employ all means in order to hasten the passage of those unfortunates. General Eblé, accompanied by some officers, himself went to their bivouacs and implored them to flee, emphasizing that he was going to destroy the bridges. But it was in vain; lying comfortably on straw or branches around great fires, devouring horse meat, they were afraid of the crowding on the bridge during the night, they hesitated to give up a sure bivouac for an uncertain one, they feared that the frost, which was very severe, would kill them in their enfeebled condition.

Napoleon's orders to General Eblé was to destroy the bridges at 7 o'clock in the morning of November 29th., but this noble man, as humane as he was brave, hesitated. He had been awake that night, the sixth of these vigils in succession, incessantly trying to accelerate the passing of the bridge; with daybreak, however, there was no need any more to stimulate the unfortunates, they all were only too anxious now. They all ran when the enemy became visible on the heights.

Eblé had waited till 8 o'clock when the order for the destruction of the bridges was repeated to him, and in sight of the approaching enemy it was his duty not to lose one moment. However, trusting to the artillery of Victor, he still tried to save some people. His soul suffered cruelly during this time of hesitation to execute an order the necessity of which he knew only too well. Finally, having waited until almost 9 o'clock when the enemy approached on the double quick, he decided with broken heart, turning his eyes away from the frightful scene, to set fire to the structures. Those unfortunates who were on the bridges threw themselves into the water, every one made a supreme effort to escape the Cossacks or captivity, which latter they feared more than death.

The Cossacks came up galloping, thrusting their lances into the midst of the crowd; they killed some, gathered the others, and drove them forward, like a herd of sheep, toward the Russian army. It is not exactly known if there were six thousand, seven thousand or eight thousand individuals, men, women, and children, who were taken by the Cossacks.

The army was profoundly affected by this spectacle and nobody more so than General Eblé who, in devoting himself to the salvation of all, could well say that he was the saviour of all who had not perished or been taken prisoner in the days of the Beresina. Of the fifty thousand, armed or unarmed, who had crossed there was not a single one who did not owe his life and liberty to him and his pontooneers. But the 400 pontooneers who had worked in the water, paid with their lives for this noblest deed in the history of wars; they all died within a short time. General Eblé survived his act of bravery only three weeks; he died in Koenigsberg on the 21st day of December, 1812.

This is an incomplete sketch of the immortal event of the Beresina, full of psychological interest and therefore fit to be inserted in the medical history of Napoleon's campaign in Russia.

To a miraculous accident, the arrival of Corbineau, the noble devotedness of Eblé, the desperate resistance of Victor and his soldiers, to the energy of Oudinot, Ney, Legrand, Maison, Zayonchek, Doumerc, and, finally, to his own sure and profound decision, his recognition of the true steps to be taken, Napoleon owed the possibility that he could escape after a bloody scene, the most humiliating, the most crushing disaster.

Two Episodes

Surgeon Huber of the Wuerttembergians, writes to his friend, Surgeon Henri de Roos, who settled in Russia after the campaign of 1812, how he crossed the Beresina, and in this connection he describes the following dreadful episode:

A young woman of twenty-five, the wife of a French colonel killed a few days before in one of the engagements, was near me, within a short distance of the bridge we were to cross. Oblivious of all that went on about her, she seemed wholly engrossed in her daughter, a beautiful child of four, that she held in the saddle before her. She made several unsuccessful attempts to cross the bridge and was driven back every time, at which she seemed overwhelmed with blank despair. She did not weep; she would gaze heavenward, then fix her eyes upon her daughter, and once I heard her say: 'O God, how wretched I am, I cannot even pray!' Almost at the same moment a bullet struck her horse and another one penetrated her left thigh above the knee. With the deliberation of mute despair she took up the child that was crying, kissed it again and again; then, using the bloodstained garter removed from her fractured limb, she strangled the poor little thing and sat down with it, wrapped in her arms and hugged close to her bosom, beside her fallen horse. Thus she awaited her end, without uttering a single word, and before long she was trampled down by the riders making for the bridge.

The great surgeon Larrey tells how he nearly perished at the crossing of the Beresina, how he went over the bridge twice to save his equipment and surgical instruments, and how he was vainly attempting to break through the crowd on the third trip, when, at the mention of his name, every one proffered assistance, and he was carried along by soldier after soldier to the end of the bridge.

He has related the incident in a letter to his wife, dated from Leipzig, March 11th., 1813. "Ribes, (Ribes was one of Napoleon's physicians), was right when he said that in the midst of the army, and especially of the Imperial guard, I could not lose my life. Indeed, I owe my life to the soldiers. Some of them flew to my rescue when the Cossacks surrounded me and would have killed or taken me prisoner. Others hastened to lift me and help me on when I sank in the snow from physical exhaustion. Others, again, seeing me suffer from hunger, gave me such provisions as they had; while as soon as I joined their bivouac they would all make room and cover me with straw or with their own clothes."

At Larrey's name, all the soldiers would rise and cheer with a friendly respect. Larrey further writes:

Anyone else in my place would have perished on the bridge of the Beresina, crossing it as I was doing, for the third time and at the most dangerous moment. But no sooner did they recognize me than they grasped me with a vigorous hold, and sent me along from hand to hand, like a bundle of clothes, to the end of the bridge.

Wilna

The threatening barrier had been surmounted, and on went the march to Wilna, without any possibility of a day's rest, because the miserable remainder of the French Army was still followed by light Russian troops.

During the first days after the crossing of the Beresina the supply of food had improved, it was better indeed than at any time during the retreat. They passed through villages which had not suffered from the war, in which the barns were well filled with grain and with feed for the horses, and there lived rich Jews who could sell whatever the soldiers needed. Unfortunately, however, this improved condition lasted only a few days, from November 30th to December 4th, and before Wilna was reached the want was felt again and made itself felt the more on account of the most intense cold which had set in.

During the few good days the soldiers had eaten roast pork, and all kinds of vegetables, in consequence their weakened digestive tract had been overtaxed so that diarrhoea became prevalent, a most frightful condition during a march on the road, with a temperature of 25 deg. below zero, Reaumur (about 25 deg. below zero, Fahrenheit).

The 6th of December was a frightful day, although the cold had not yet reached its climax which happened on the 7th and 8th of December, namely 28 deg. below zero, Reaumur (31 degrees below zero, Fahrenheit).

Holzhausen gives a graphic description of the supernatural silence which reigned and which reminded of the silence in the arctic regions. There was not the slightest breeze, the snowflakes fell vertically, crystal-clear, the snow blinded the eyes, the sun appeared like a red hot ball with a halo, the sign of greatest cold.

The details of the descriptions which Holzhausen has collected from old papers surpass by far all we have learned from von Scherer's

"THE GATE OF WILNA."

and Beaupré's writings. And all that Holzhausen relates is verified by names of absolute reliability; it verifies the accounts of the two authors named.

General von Roeder, one of the noblest of the German officers in Napoleon's army—a facsimile of one of his letters is given in Holzhausen's book—says about the murderous 7th of December:

> Pilgrims of the Grand Army, who had withstood many a severe frost indeed, dropped like flies, and of those who were well nourished, well clothed—many of these being of the reserve corps having but recently come from Wilna to join the retreating army,—countless numbers fell exactly like the old exhausted warriors who had dragged themselves from Moscow to this place.

The reserve troops of which Roeder speaks were the division Loison, the last great body of men that had followed the army. They had been in Koenigsberg and had marched from there to Wilna during the month of November, had remained in the latter place until December 4th, when they were sent to protect the retreating soldiers and the Emperor himself, on leaving the wreck of his once grand army at Smorgoni on December 5th.

These troops who thus far had not sustained any hardships, came directly from the warm quarters of Wilna into the terrible cold. Roeder says:

> It was quite frightful to see these men, who a moment before had been talking quite lively, drop dead as if struck by lightning.

D. Geissler, a Weimaranian surgeon, renders a similar report and adds that in some cases these victims suffered untold agonies before they died.

Lieutenant Jacobs states that some said goodbye to their comrades and laid down along the road to die, that others acted like maniacs, cursed their fate, fell down, rose again, and fell down once more, never to rise again. Cases like the latter have been described also by First Lieutenant von Schauroth. Holzhausen says:

> Under these circumstances, it appears almost incomprehensible that there were men who withstood a misery which surpassed all human dimensions.

And still there were such; who by manfully bearing these sufferings, set to others a good example; there were whole troops who, to protect others in pertinacious rear guard fights, opposed the on-pressing enemy.

Wonderful examples of courage and self-denial gave some women, the wife of a Sergeant-Major Martens, who had followed the army, and a Mrs. Basler, who was always active, preparing some food while her husband with others was lying exhausted at the camp fire, and who seldom spoke, never complained. This poor woman lost a son, a drummer boy, who had been wounded at Smolensk. She as well as her husband perished in Wilna.

Sergeant Toenges dragged a blind comrade along—"I shall not leave him," he said. Grenadiers, sitting around a fire, had pity on him and tried to relieve his sufferings. Many such examples are enumerated in Holzhausen's book.

Our highest admiration is due to the conduct of the brave troops of the rear guard who fought the Russians, who sacrificed themselves for the sake of the whole, and, like at Krasnoe and at the Beresina, for their disbanded comrades.

The rearguard was at first commanded by Ney, then, after the 3rd of December, by Marshal Victor; after the dissolution of Victor's corps at Smorgoni and Krapowna, by Loison and, finally, near Wilna, by Wrede with his Bavarians.

Count Hochberg has given a classical description of the life in the rear guard; it is the most elevating description of greatness, of human magnanimity, and it fills us with admiration for the noble, the brave soldier.

Interesting is the engagement at Malodeszno. A certain spell hangs over this fight; here perished two Saxon regiments that had gloriously fought at the Beresina.

The scene was a romantic park with the castle of Count Oginsky where Napoleon had had his headquarters on the preceding day, and from where he dated his forever memorable 29th bulletin in which he told the world the ruin of his army.

Toward 2 o'clock in the afternoon the enemy attacked the division of Girard who was supported by Count Hochberg. Then the Russians attacked the park itself. The situation was very serious, because the Badensian troops under Hochberg had only a few cartridges and could not properly answer the fire of the enemy. Night came, and the darkness, writes a Badensian sergeant, was of great advantage to us, for the Russians stood against a very small number, the proportion being one battalion to 100 men. Count Hochberg led his brigade, attacking with the bayonet, and nearly became a victim of his courage. The Badensian troops drove the enemy away, but they themselves received the death blow. Count Hochberg said he had no soldiers left whom he could command.

And now it was the division Loison which formed the rear guard.

On the 5th of December this division had come to Smorgoni where Napoleon took leave from his marshals and from his army, after he had entrusted Murat with the command.

The division Loison, during the eventful night from December 5th. to 6th., had rendered great services. Without the presence of Loison's soldiers Napoleon would have fallen into the hands of his enemies, and the wheel of the history of the world would have taken a different turn.

Dr. Geissler describes Napoleon, whom he saw at a few paces' distance on the day of his departure, and he writes:

The personality of this extraordinary man, his physiognomy with the stamp of supreme originality, the remembrance of his powerful deeds by which he moved the world during his time, carried us away in involuntary admiration. Was not the voice which we heard the same which resounded all over Europe, which declared wars, decided battles, regulated the fate of empires, elevated or extinguished the glory of so many.

It may appear strange that in a medical history I record these details, but I give them because they show how the personality of Napoleon had retained its magic influence even in that critical moment.

The soldiers wanted to salute him with their *Vive l'Empereur*! but, in consideration of the assumed *incognito* of the *imperator* without an army, it was interdicted.

Up to this day Napoleon has been blamed for his step, to leave the army. At the Beresina he had refused with pride the offer of some Poles to take him over the river and to bring him safely to Wilna. Now there was nothing more to save of the army, and other duties called him peremptorily away. If we study well the situation, the complications which had arisen from the catastrophe and which were to arise in the following year, we must in justice to him admit that he was obliged to go in order to create another army.

It is not a complete history which I am writing; otherwise it would be my duty to speak of the deep impression, the dramatic effect, which Napoleon's departure had made on his soldiers. In presenting somewhat extensively some details of those days I simply wished to show who they were and how many brave men there were who had been spared for the atrocities of Wilna.

If I were to do justice to the voluminous material before me of the bravery of the soldiers on their march from the Beresina to Wilna I would have to write a whole book on this part of the history alone.

★★★★★★

Once more the hope of the unfortunates should be disappointed in a most cruel way. They knew of fresh troops and of rich magazines in Wilna. But only two thousand men were left of the Loison division, not enough to defend the place against the enemy whose coming was to be expected.

The provisions, however, were stored in the magazines, and there were, according to French accounts, forty day rations of bread, flour and crackers for 100 thousand men, cattle for 36 days, nine million rations of wine and brandy; in addition, vegetables and food for horses, as well as clothing in abundance.

Unfortunately, the governor of Wilna, the Duke of Bassano, was only a diplomat, entirely incompetent to handle the situation, which required military talent.

Unfortunate had also been Napoleon's choice of Murat. On August 31st, 1817, he said in conversation with Gourgaud, "I have made a great mistake in entrusting Murat with the highest command of the army, because he was the most incompetent man to act successfully under such circumstances."

No preparations were made for the entering troops, no quarters had been assigned for them when they came.

And they came on the 9th; most horrible details have been recorded of this day when the disbanded mass crowded the gate.

Wilna was not only not in ruins, but it was the only large city which had not been abandoned by its inhabitants. But these inhabitants shut their doors before the entering soldiers. Only some officers and some Germans, the latter among the families of German mechanics, found an abode in the houses. Some Poles were hospitable, also some Lithuanians, and even the Jews.

All writers complain of the avidity and cruelty of the latter; they mixed among the soldiers to obtain whatever they had saved from the pillage of Moscow. These Jews had everything the soldier was in need of, bread and brandy, delicacies and even horses and sleighs; in their restaurants all who had money or valuables could be accommodated. And these places were crowded with soldiers who feasted at the well supplied tables, and even hilarity developed among these men saved from the ice fields of Russia. During the night every space was occupied as a resting place.

While those who could afford it enjoyed all the good things of which they had been deprived so long, the poor soldiers in the streets were in great misery. The doors being shut, they entered the houses by force and ill-treated the inhabitants who on the next day took a bitter revenge.

Even the rich magazines had remained closed, tedious formalities had to be observed, the carrying out of which was an impossibility since the whole army was disbanded. No regiment had kept together, no detachment could be selected to present vouchers for receiving rations.

Lieutenant Jacobs gives an illustration of the condition:

Orders had been given to receive rations for four days. Colonel von Egloffstein in the evening of the 9th sent Lieutenant Jacobs with 100 men to the bread magazine to secure as much as possible, and as this magazine was at some distance, and as Cossacks had already entered the city, he ordered 25 armed men to accompany the hundred, who, naturally enough, were not armed. The commissary of the magazine refused to hand out bread without a written order of the *commissaire-ordonateur*; the lieutenant therefore notified him that he would take by force what he needed for his regiment. And with his twenty-five *carabiniers* he had to fight for the bread.

Finally the pressing need led to violence. During the night of the 10th the desperate soldiers, aided by inhabitants, broke into the magazines, at first into those containing clothing, then they opened the provision stores, throwing flour bags and loaves of bread into the street where the masses fought for these missiles. And when the liquor depots were broken into, the crowd forced its way in with howls. They broke the barrels, and wild orgies took place until the building took fire and many of the revellers became the victims of the flames.

While this pillaging went on the market place of Wilna was the scene of events not less frightful. A detachment of Loison's division, obedient to their duty, had congregated there, stacked arms and, in order to warm themselves to the best of their ability—the temperature was 30 deg. below zero R. (37 deg. below zero F.)—and to thaw the frozen bread, had lighted a fire. I cannot describe the fight among these soldiers for single pieces of bread; they were too horrid.

This night ended, and in the morning the cannon was heard again.

An early attack had been expected, and perspicacious officers had taken advantage of the few hours of rest to urge their men to prepare for the last march to the near frontier. Count Hochberg implored his officers to follow this advice, but the fatigues and sickness they had undergone, their frozen limbs and the threat of greater misery, made most of them refuse to heed his entreaties. Thus Hochberg lost 74 of his best and most useful officers who remained in Wilna and died there. Similar attempts were made in other quarters. Many of those addressed laughed sneeringly. This sneering I shall never forget, says Lieutenant von Hailbronner, who escaped while the enemy was entering. Death on the road to Kowno was easier, after all, than dying slowly in the hospitals of Wilna.

On the 10th., in the morning, the Russians entered, and the Cossacks ran their lances through every one in their way.

There were fights in the streets, the troops of the division Loison fought the Russians.

Old Sergeant Picart, of the old guard, on hearing the drum, struck his comrade Bourgogne, the writer of some memoirs of the campaign, on the shoulder, saying: "Forward, comrade, we are of the old guard, we must be the first under arms." And Bourgogne went along, although sick and wounded.

German and French bravery vied with each other on the 10th of December. Ney and Loison along with Wrede. The latter, on the day previous, had come to the house of the marshal to offer him a small escort of cavalry if he would leave Wilna. Ney pointing to the mass of soldiers who had to be protected, answered: "All the Cossacks in the world shall not bring me out of this city tonight."

Ney and Wrede left with their troops.

Woe to those who had remained, their number was about ten thousand, besides five thousand sick in the hospitals.

According to Roeder, 500 were murdered in the streets on this day, partly by Cossacks, partly by Jews, the latter revenging themselves for ill treatment.

All reports, and they are numerous, of Germans, French and also

In the streets of Wilna

Russians, speak of the cruelty of the Jews of Wilna. We must not forget, however, the provocations under which they had to suffer, nor how they, in supplying soldiers with eatables and clothing, saved many who otherwise would have perished.

Von Lossberg says that Christian people of Wilna have also taken part in the massacre, and only the Poles did not participate.

The Cossacks began their bloody work early in the morning.

Awful cries of the tortured were heard in the Wuerttembergian hospital, telling the sick who were lying there what they themselves had to expect from the entering enemies.

Those who had remained in Smolensk and Moscow after the armed soldiers had departed were at once massacred. In Wilna likewise many were murdered, but the greater number—many thousands—(other circumstances did not permit to do away with all these prisoners in the same way) perished after days or weeks of sickness and privations of all kind.

Wilna's convents could tell of it if their walls could speak.

Dr. Geissler narrates that the prisoners in the Basilius monastery into which soldiers of all nationalities had been driven, during thirteen days received only a little hardtack, but neither wood nor a drop of water; they had to quench their thirst with the snow which covered the corpses in the yard.

The Englishman Wilson, of whom I have spoken already, who had come to Wilna with Kutusow's army, says:

The Basilius monastery, transformed into a prison, offered a terrible sight—7,500 corpses were piled up in the corridors, and corpses were also in other parts of the building, the broken windows and the holes in the walls were plugged with feet, legs, hands, heads, trunks, just as they would fit in the openings to keep out the cold air. The putrefying flesh spread a terrible stench.

(Carpon, a French Surgeon-Major who was with the army in Wilna, has described the events in a paper *Les Morts de Wilna*. I cannot quote from his writings because he gives impossible statistics and contradicts himself in his narrations.)

Yelin speaks of a hospital in which all the inmates had been murdered by the Cossacks. He himself was in a Wuerttembergian hospital and describes his experience:

Terrible was the moment when the door was burst open. The

monsters came in and distributed themselves all over the house. We gave them all we had and implored them on our knees to have pity, but all in vain. '*Schelma Franzuski,*' they answered, at the same time they beat us with their *kantchous*, kicked us unmercifully with their feet, and as new Cossacks came in all the time, we were finally deprived of all our clothing and beaten like dogs. Even the bandages of the poor wounded were torn off in search of hidden money or valuables. Lieutenant Kuhn (a piece of his cranium had been torn away at Borodino) was searched; he fell down like dead and it took a long time and much pain to bring him to life again.

Lieutenant von Soden was beaten with hellish cruelty on his sore feet and gangrenous toes so that they bled. When nothing more could be found on the sick and wounded they were left lying on the stone floor.

There was no idea of medicine.

The cold in the rooms was so great that hands and feet of many were frozen.

Sometimes prisoners shaking with frost would sneak out at night to find a little wood. Some Westphalians who had tried this were beaten to death.

Some of the prisoners were literally eaten up by lice.

Those who did not die of their wounds, of filth, and of misery, were carried away by petechial typhus which had developed into a violent epidemic in Wilna, and several thousand of the citizens, among them many Jews, succumbed to the ravages of this disease.

One witness writes:

"Little ceremony was observed in disposing of the dead; every morning I heard how those who had died during the night were thrown down the stairs or over the balcony into the yard, and by counting these sinister sounds of falling bodies we knew how many had died during the night."

The brutality of the guards was beyond description. First Lieutenant von Grolman, one of the most highly educated officers of the Badensian contingent, was thrown down the stairway because this (seriously wounded) officer had disturbed the inspector during the latter's leisure hour.

Beating with the *kantchou* was nothing unusual.

A Weimaranian musician, Theuss, has described some guileful tortures practiced on the prisoners, which are so revolting that I dare not write them. They are given in Holzhausen's book.

In their despair the prisoners, especially the officers among them, sent petitions to Duke Alexander of Wuerttemberg, to the *Tzar*, to the Grand Duke Constantine, and to the ladies of the Russian Court. The *Tzar* and his brother Constantine came and visited the hospitals. They were struck by what they saw, and ordered relief. Officers were permitted to walk about the city, and many obtained quarters in private houses. Those who could not yet leave the gloomy wards of the hospitals were better cared for.

It is touching to read Yelin's narration how the emaciated arms of those in the hospitals were stretched out when their comrades, returning from a promenade in the city, brought them a few apples.

As they were no longer guarded as closely as before, many succeeded in escaping. Captain Roeder was one of them; Yelin was offered aid to flee, but he remained because he had given his word of honour to remain.

But most of these favours came too late, only one tenth were left that could be saved, the others had succumbed to their sufferings or died from typhus.

A pestilential odour filled Wilna. Heaps of cadavers were burnt and when this was found to be too expensive, thrown into the Wilia. Few of the higher officers were laid at rest in the cemetery, among them General von Roeder who as long as he was able had tried everything in his power to ameliorate the condition of his soldiers. Holzhausen brings the facsimile of a letter of his, dated Wilna, December 30th, to the King of Wuerttemberg which proves his care for his soldiers. He died on January 6th, 1813.

From Wilna to Kowno

While the prisoners of Wilna were suffering these nameless cruelties, the unfortunate army marched to reach the border of Russia at
Kowno, the same Kowno where the Grand Army six months before
had been seen in all its military splendour, crossing the Niemen.

They had now to march 75 miles, a three days' march to arrive
there.

The conditions were about the same as those on the march from
the Beresina to Wilna. Still the same misery, frost, and hunger, scenes
of murder, fire. The description of the details would in general be a
repetition, with little variation.

The following is an account of the last days of the retreat taken
from a letter of Berthier to the emperor.

> When the army entered Wilna on December 8th, almost all
> the men were chilled by cold, and despite the commands of
> Murat and Berthier, despite the fact that the Russians were at
> the gates, both officers and soldiers kept to their quarters and
> refused to march.
>
> However, on the 10th, the march upon Kowno was begun. But
> the extreme cold and the excess of snow completed the rout of
> the army. The final disbanding occurred on the 10th, and 11th,
> only a struggling column remained, extending along the road,
> strewn with corpses, setting out at daybreak to halt at night in
> utter confusion. In fact, there was no army left. How could it
> have subsisted with 25 degrees of cold? The onslaught, alas, was
> not of the foe, but of the harshest and severest of seasons fraught
> with crippling effect and untold suffering.

Berthier, as well as Murat, would have wished to remain in Kowno
through the 12th, but the disorder was extreme. Houses were pillaged

and sacked, half the town was burned down, the Niemen was being crossed at all points, and it was impossible to stem the tide of fugitives. An escort was barely available for the protection of the King of Naples, the generals, and the Imperial eagles. And all amidst the cold, the intense cold, stupefying and benumbing!

Four fifths of the army—or what bore the name of such, though reduced to a mere conglomeration and bereft of fighting men—had frozen limbs; and when Koenigsberg was reached, in a state of complete disorganisation, the surgeons were constantly employed in amputating fingers and toes.

Dr. W. Zelle, a German military surgeon, in his book *1812* describes the last days of the army. Kowno was occupied by a considerable force of artillery, with two German battalions, and it contained also very large supplies, a great deal of ammunition, provisions, clothing, and arms of various kinds. About an hour's march from Wilna the retreating masses encountered the hill and defile of Ponary and it was at this point where the imperial treasure, so far conscientiously guarded by German troops from Baden and Wuerttemberg, was lost. When the leaders of the treasure became convinced of the impossibility to save it, the jaded horses not being able after 15 hours' effort to climb the ice covered hill, they had the wagons opened, the money chests broken, and the coin surrendered to the soldiers.

The sight of the gold brought new life even to the half frozen ones; they threw away their arms and were so greedy in loading themselves down with the mammon that many of them did not notice the approaching Cossacks until it was too late. Friend and foe, Frenchmen and Russians pillaged the wagons. Honour, money, and what little had remained of discipline, all was lost at this point.

However, side by side with these outrages, noble deeds could also be recorded. Numerous wagons with wounded officers had to be abandoned, the horses being too weak to take another step, and many of the soldiers disregarded everything to save these unfortunates, carrying them away on their shoulders. An adjutant of the emperor, Count Turenne, distributed the private treasure of the emperor among the soldiers of the Old Guard, and not one of these faithful men kept any of the money for himself. All was honestly returned later on, and more than 6 millions of *francs* reached Danzig safely.

The retreat during these scenes and the following days, when the terrible cold caused more victims from hour to hour, was still covered by Ney whose iron constitution defied all hardships. From five until

RETREAT ACROSS THE NIEMAN

ten at night he personally checked the advance of the enemy, during the night he marched, driving all stragglers before him. From seven in the morning until ten the rear guard rested, after which time they continued the daily fight.

His Bavarians numbered 260 on December 11th, 150 on the 17th and on the 13th the last twenty were taken prisoners. The corps had disappeared. The remainder of Loison's division and the garrison of Wilna diminished in the same manner until, finally, the rear guard consisted of only sixty men.

What was left of the army reached Kowno on the 12th, after a long, tedious march, dying of cold and hunger. In Kowno there was an abundance of clothes, flour, and spirits. But the unrestrained soldiers broke the barrels, so that the spilled liquor formed a lake in the market place. The soldiers threw themselves down and by the hundreds drank until they were intoxicated. More than 1200 drunken men reeled through the streets, dropped drowsily upon the icy stones or into the snow, their sleep soon passing into death. Of the entire corps of Eugene there remained only eight or ten officers with the prince.

Only one day more (the 13th) was the powerful Ney able, with the two German battalions of the garrison, to check the Cossacks, vigorously supported by the indefatigable generals, Gerard and Wrede. Not until the 14th, at 9 o'clock at night, did he begin to retreat, with the last of the men, after having destroyed the bridges over the Wilia and the Niemen. Always fighting, receding but not fleeing, his person formed the rear guard of this Grand Army which five months previous crossed the river at this very point, now, on the 14th, consisting of only 500 foot guards, 600 horse guards, and nine cannon.

It is nobody but Ney who still represents the Grand Army, who fires the last shot before he, the last Frenchman, crosses the bridge over the Niemen, which is blown up behind him. If we look upon the knightly conduct of Ney during the entire campaign we cannot but think how much greater he was than the heroes of Homer.

This man has demonstrated to the world upon this most terrible of all retreats that even fate is not able to subdue an imperturbable courage, that even the greatest adversity redounds to the glory of a hero.

More than a thousand times did Ney earn in Russia the epithet, "*the bravest of the brave*," and the legend which French tradition has woven around his person is quite justified. No mortal has ever performed such deeds of indomitable moral courage; all other heroes and exploits vanish in comparison!

Here, at the Niemen, the pursuit by the Russians came to an end for the time being. They, too, had suffered enormously.

Not less than eighteen thousand Russians were sick in Wilna; Kutusoff's army was reduced to thirty-five thousand men, that of Wittgenstein from fifty thousand to fifteen thousand. The entire Russian Army, including the garrison of Riga, numbered not more than 100 thousand. The winter, this terrible ally of the Russians, exacted a high price for the assistance it had rendered them; of ten thousand men who left the interior, well provided with all necessities, only 1700 reached Wilna; the troops of cavalry did not number more than twenty men.

In all the literature which I have examined I did not find a better description of the life and the struggle of the soldiers on the retreat than that given by General Heinrich von Brandt of his march from Zembin to Wilna. It is a vivid picture of many details from which we derive a full understanding of the great misery on the retreat in general.

I shall give an extensive extract in his own words:

"We arrived late at Zembin, where we found many bivouac fires. It was very cold. Here and there around the fires were lying dead soldiers.

After a short rest, which had given us some new strength, we continued the march. If the stragglers arrive, we said to ourselves, we shall be lost; therefore, let us hurry and keep ahead of them. Our little column kept well together, but at every halt some men were missing. Toward daybreak the cold became more severe. While it was dark yet, we met a file of gunpowder carts carrying wounded; from a number of these vehicles we heard heart-rending clamours of some of the wounded asking us to give them death.

At every moment we encountered dead or dying comrades, officers and soldiers, who were sitting on the road, exhausted from fatigue, awaiting their end. The sun rose blood-red; the cold was frightful. We stopped near a village where bivouac fires were burning. Around these fires were grouped living and dead soldiers. We lodged ourselves as well as we could and took from those who had retired from the scene of life—apparently during their sleep—anything that could be of service to us. I for my part helped myself to a pot in which I melted snow to make a soup from some bread crusts which I had in my pocket.

We all relished this soup.

After an hour's rest we resumed our march and about thirty hours after our departure we reached Plechtchenissi. During this time we had made twenty-five miles. At Plechtchenissi we found, at a kind of farm, sick, wounded and dead, all lying pell-mell. There was no room for us in the house; we were obliged to camp outside, but great fires compensated us for the want of shelter.

We decided to rest during part of the night. While some of the soldiers roasted slices of horse meat and others prepared oatmeal cakes from oats which they had found in the village, we tried to sleep. But the frightful scenes through which we had passed kept us excited, and sleep would not come.

Toward 1 o'clock in the morning we left for Molodetchno. The cold was frightful. Our way was marked by the light of the bivouac fires which were seen at intervals and by cadavers of men and horses lying everywhere, and as the moon and the stars were out we could see them well. Our column became smaller all the while, officers and men disappeared without our noticing their departure, without our knowing where they had fallen behind; and the cold increased constantly.

When we stopped at some bivouac fire it seemed to us as if we were among the dead; nobody stirred, only occasionally would one or the other of those sitting around raise his head, look upon us with glassy eyes, rest again, probably never to rise again. What made the march during that night especially disagreeable was the icy wind whipping our faces. Toward 8 o'clock in the morning we perceived a church tower. That is Molodetchno, we all cried with one voice. But to our disappointment we learned on our arrival that it was only Iliya, and that we were only half-way to Molodetchno.

Iliya was not completely deserted by the inhabitants, but the troops that had passed through it before us had left almost nothing eatable in the place. We found abode in some houses and for a while were protected from the cold which was by no means abating. In the farm of which we took possession we found a warm room and a good litter, which we owed to our predecessors.

It was strange that none of us could sleep; we all were in a state of feverish excitement, and I attribute this to an indistinct fear;

once asleep we might perhaps not awake again, as we had seen it happen a thousand times.

The longer we remained at Iliya the more comfortable we felt, and we decided to stay there all day and wait for news. Soup of buckwheat, a large pot of boiled corn, some slices of roast horse meat, although all without salt, formed a meal which we thought delicious.

Von Brandt describes how they took off their garments, or their wrappings which served as garments, to clean and repair them; how some of his men found leather with which they enveloped their feet. The day and the night passed, and all had some sleep. But they had to leave.

Some of the men refused to go; one of them when urged to come along said: 'Captain, let me die here; we all are to perish, a few days sooner or later is of no consequence.' He was wounded, but not seriously, a bullet had passed through his arm; it was a kind of apathy which had come over him, and he could not be persuaded. He remained and probably died.

We left; the cold was almost unbearable. Along the road we found bivouacs, at which one detachment relieved the other; the succeeding surpassing the preceding one in misery and distress. Everywhere, on the road and in the bivouacs, the dead were lying, most of them stripped of their clothes.

It was imperative to keep moving, for remaining too long at the bivouac fires meant death, and dangerous was it also to remain behind, separated from the troop. (The danger of being alone under such circumstances as existed here has been pointed out by Beaupré.)

We marched to Molodetchno where the great road commences and where we expected some amelioration, and, indeed, we found it. The everlasting cold was now the principal cause of our sufferings.

In the village there was some kind of order; we saw many soldiers bearing arms and of a general good appearance. The houses were not all deserted, neither were they as overcrowded as in other places through which we had passed. We established ourselves in some of them situated on the road to Smorgoni, and we had reason to be satisfied with our choice. We bought bread at an enormous price, made soup of it which tasted very good to us, and we had plenty for all of us.

At Molodetchno men of our division joined us and brought us the news of the crossing of the Beresina.

Von Brandt gives the description of the events at the Beresina and tells of the historical significance of Molodetchno as the place where Napoleon sojourned 18 hours and from where he dated the 29th bulletin.

We left the village on the following morning at an early hour and continued our march on the road to Smorgoni.

A description of this march would only be a repetition of what had been said of scenes of preceding days. We were overtaken by a snowstorm the violence of which surpassed all imagination, fortunately this violence lasted only some hours, but on account of it our little column became dispersed.

One bivouac left an impression of horror to last for all my lifetime. In a village crowded with soldiers we came to a fire which was burning quite lively, around it were lying some dead. We were tired; it was late, and we decided to rest there. We removed the corpses to make room for the living and arranged ourselves the best way we could. A fence against which the snow had drifted protected us from the north wind.

Many who passed by envied us this good place. Some stopped for a while, others tried to establish themselves near us. Gradually the fatigue brought sleep to some of us; the stronger ones brought wood to keep up the fire. But it snowed constantly; after one had warmed one side of the body an effort was made to warm the other; after one foot had been warmed the other was brought near the flame; a complete rest was impossible. At daybreak we prepared to depart. Thirteen men of our troop, all wounded, did not answer the roll call. My heart pained.

We had to pass in front of the fence which had given us protection against the wind during the night. Imagine our surprise when we saw that what we had taken for a fence was a pile of corpses which our predecessors had heaped one upon the other. These dead were men of all countries, Frenchmen, Swiss, Italians, Poles, Germans, as we could distinguish by their uniforms. Most of them had their arms extended as if they had been stretching themselves. 'Look, captain,' said one of the soldiers, 'they stretch their hands out to us; ah, no fear, we soon

"No fear, we soon shall follow you."

shall follow you.'

We were soon to have another horrid sight. In a village, many houses of which had been burnt, there were the ghastly remains of burnt corpses, and in one building, especially, there was a large number of such infesting the air with their stench. A repetition of scenes I had seen at Saragossa and at Smolensk."

At sunset we arrived at Smorgoni, and here we enjoyed great comfort. It was the first place where we could obtain something for money. From an old Jewess we bought bread, rice, and also a little coffee, all at reasonable prices. It was the first cup of coffee I had had for months, and it invigorated me very much. We were young, and our good humour had soon been restored to us; it made us forget, for the time being at least, how much we had suffered, and at this moment we did not think of the suffering yet in store for us.

We left for Ochmiana; our march was tedious. Again we encountered a great many dead strewn on the road; many of them had died from cold; some still had their arms, young men, well dressed, their cloaks, shoes, and socks, however, were taken from them. Halfway to Ochmiana we took a rest at a bivouac which had been evacuated quite recently.

The night we passed here was fearful. I had an inflamed foot, and felt a burning pain under the arms which caused me great difficulty in the use of my crutches. Fortunately I found a place on which a fire had been burning, and I was not obliged to sleep on the snow. The soldiers kept up a fire all night, and I had a good and invigorating sleep, in consequence of which I could take up the march on the following day, with new courage and zeal.

Toward 11 o'clock we arrived, together with a mass of fugitives, at Ochmiana. Before entering the city we encountered a convoy of provisions, escorted by a young Mecklenburg officer, Lieutenant Rudloff, who some years later served as a Prussian general. He made an attempt to defend his sleighs, but in vain. The crowd surrounded him and his convoy and pushed in such a manner that neither he nor his men were able to stir. The sleighs, carrying excellent biscuits, were pillaged. I myself gathered some in the snow, and I can well say that they saved my life until we reached Wilna.

Arrived at Ochmiana we at once continued our march upon

Miednicki.

The city was occupied by a crowd of disbanded soldiers—marauders who had established themselves everywhere. It was only with difficulty that we found some sort of lodging in a kind of pavilion which was icy and had no chimneys. However, we managed to heat it and arranged litter for twenty men. With bread and biscuit brought from Ochmiana we prepared a good meal.

When we crossed the Goina we numbered fifty; this number had increased so that we were at one time seventy, but now our number had decreased to twenty-nine.

We left at an early hour on the next morning. It was frightfully cold. Half way to Miednicki we had to stop at a bivouac. On the road we saw many cadavers.

Von Brandt here describes the fatal effects of cold and his description, though less complete, corresponds with the descriptions given by Beaupré, von Scherer, and others. Especially revolting, he says, was the sight of the toes of the cadavers; often there were no more soft parts. The soldiers, first of all, took the shoes from their dead comrades, next the cloaks; they would wear two or three or cut one to cover their feet and their head with the pieces.

The last part of the march to Miedniki was most painful for von Brandt, on account of the inflammation of his left foot.

He describes his stay at that place in which there were many stragglers. He bivouacked in a garden; they had straw enough and a good fire, also biscuits from Ochmiana, and they suffered only from the cold, 30 deg. below zero R. (36 deg. below zero Fahrenheit.) On this occasion von Brandt speaks of the pains, the sufferings, the condition of his comrades. One of them, Zelinski, had not uttered a word since their departure from Smorgoni; he had no tobacco, and this troubled him more than physical pain; another one, Karpisz, crushed by sorrow and sufferings, was in a delirious state; in the same condition were some of the wounded. But after all, in the midst of their sad reflections, some of them fell asleep. Those who were well enough took up reliefs on night watch.

Every one of the group had to bear some special great misery, and upon the whole their trials were beyond endurance: In the open air at 30 deg. R. below zero, without sufficient clothing, without provisions, full of vermin, exposed at any moment to the attacks of the enemy, surrounded by a rapacious rabble, deprived of aid, wounded, they were hardly in a condition to drag themselves along.

"Still an 8 hours' march to Wilna," I said to Zelinski; "Will we reach there?" He shook his head in doubt.

One of the men, Wasilenka, a sergeant, the most courageous, the firmest of the little column, of a robust constitution, had found at Ochmiana some brandy and some potatoes. He said if one had not lost his head entirely, one could have many things, but nothing can be done with the French anymore; they are not the Frenchmen of former times, a Cossack's casque upsets them; it is a shame! And he told the great news of Napoleon's departure from the army of which the others of von Brandt's column had yet not been informed. Interesting as was the conversation on this event, I have to omit it.

The extreme cold did not allow much sleep; long before daylight they were on their feet. It was a morning of desolation, as always.

Von Brandt now describes the characteristic phenomena of the landscape; the words are almost identical with the description Beaupré has given of the Russian landscape in the winter of 1812.

I could not march, the pain under my shoulders was very great. I felt as if all at this region of my body would tear off. But I marched all the same. Many were already on the road, all in haste to reach the supposed end of their sufferings. They seemed to be in a race, and the cold, the incredible cold, drove them also to march quickly. On this day there perished more men than usual, and we passed these unfortunates without a sign of pity, as if all human feeling had been extinguished in the souls of us, the surviving. We marched in silence, hardly any one uttered a word; if, however, some one spoke, it was to say how is it that I am not in your place; besides this nothing was heard but the sighing and the groans of the dying.

It was perhaps 9 o'clock when we had covered half of the way and took a short rest, after which we resumed our march and arrived before Wilna toward 3 o'clock, having marched ten hours, exhausted beyond description. The cold was intolerable; as I learned afterward it had reached 29 deg. below zero Reaumur (36 deg. below zero Fahrenheit.) But imagine our surprise when armed guards forbade us to enter the city. The order had been given to admit only regular troops. The commanders had thought of the excesses of Smolensk and Orscha and here at least they intended to save the magazines from pillage. Our little column remained at the gate for a while; we saw that whoever risked to mix with the crowd could not extricate himself again and could neither advance nor return. It came near sunset, the cold by no means abated but, on the contrary, augmented.

Every minute the crowd increased in number, the dying and dead mixed up with the living. We decided to go around the city, to try to enter at some other part; after half an hour's march we succeeded and found ourselves in the streets. They were full of baggage, soldiers, and inhabitants. But where to turn? Where to seek aid? By good luck we remembered that our officers passing Wilna on their way during the spring had been well received by Mr. Malczewski, a friend of our colonel. Nothing more natural than to go to him and ask for asylum. But imagine our joy, our delight, when at our arrival at the house we found our colonel himself, the quartermaster and many officers known by us, who all were the guests of Mr. Malczewski. Even Lieutenant Gordon who commanded our depot at Thorn was there; he had come after he had had the news of the battle of Borodino.

My faithful servant Maciejowski and the brave Wasilenka carried me up the stairs and placed me in bed. I was half dead, hardly master of my senses. Gordon gave me a shirt, my servant took charge of my garments to free them from vermin, and after I had had some cups of hot beer with ginger in it and was under a warm blanket, I recovered strength enough to understand what I was told and to do what I was asked to do."

A Jewish physician examined and dressed my wounds. He found my shoulders very much inflamed and prescribed an ointment which had an excellent effect. I fell into a profound sleep which was interrupted by the most bizarre imaginary scenes; there was not one of the hideous episodes of the last fortnight which did not pass in some form or another before my mind.

Washed, cleaned, passably invigorated, refreshed especially by some cups of hot beer, I was able to rise on the following morning and to assist at the council which the colonel had called together.

Von Brandt now describes how the mass of fugitives came and pillaged the magazines. The colonel saved a great many, supplied them with shoes, cloaks, caps, woollen socks, and provisions, von Brandt describes the scenes of Wilna from the time the Cossacks had entered.

The colonel prepared to depart; at first he hesitated to take us, the wounded, along, asking if we could stand the voyage. I said to remain would be certain death, and with confidence I set out on the march with my men, the number of whom was now twenty. We had sleighs and good horses.
The night was superb. It was light like day. The stars shone more radiantly than ever upon our misery. The cold was still severe beyond description and more sensible to us who had nearly lost the habit to feel it during forty-eight hours of relief.
We had to make our way through an indescribable tangle of carriages and wagons to reach the gate, and the road as far as we could see was also covered with vehicles, wagons, sleighs, cannons, all mixed up. We had great difficulties to remain together.
After an hour's march all came to a halt; we found ourselves before a veritable sea of men. The wagons could not be drawn over a hill on account of the ice, and the road became hopelessly blockaded. Here it was where the military treasure of 12 million *francs* was given to the soldiers.

Von Brandt describes his most wonderful adventures on the way to Kowno which, although most interesting, add nothing to what has already been described. I gave this foregoing part of von Brandt's narration because it gives a most vivid picture of the life of the soldiers during the supreme moments of the retreat from Moscow.

Prisoners of War

Beaupré was taken prisoner at the passage of the Beresina and remained in captivity for some time. His lot as a prisoner of war was an exceptionally good one. He tells us that prisoners when they were out of such parts of the country as had been ravaged by the armies, received regular rations of a very good quality, and were lodged by eight, ten, and twelve, with the peasants. In the provincial capitals, they received furs of sheep skin, fur bonnets, gloves, and coarse woollen stockings, a sort of dress that appeared to them grotesque as well as novel, but which was very precious as a protection against the cold during the winter. When arrived at the places in which they were to pass the time of their captivity they found their lot ameliorated, and the reception accorded to them demanded a grateful eulogy of the hospitality exercised by the Russians.

Quite different was the experience of a very young German, Karl Schehl, a private whose memoirs have been kept in his family, and were recently published by one of his grand-nephews. After a battle on the retreat from Moscow he, with many others, was taken prisoner by Cossacks, who at once plundered the captives. Schehl was deprived of his uniform, his breeches, his boots. He had a gold ring on his ring finger, and one of the Cossacks, thinking it too much trouble to remove the ring in the natural way, had already drawn his sabre to cut off the prisoner's left hand, when an officer saw this and gave the brutal Cossack a terrible blow in the face; he then removed the ring without hurting the boy and kept it for himself. Another officer took Schehl's gold watch. Schehl stood then with no other garment but a shirt, and barefoot, in the bitter cold, not daring to approach the bivouac fire.

The Cossacks (on examining the garments of Schehl), found in one of the pockets a B clarinet. This discovery gave them great pleasure; they induced their captive to play for them, and he played, chilled

128

In prison

to the bone in his scanty costume. But now the Cossacks came to offer him garments, a regular outfit for the Russian winter. They gave him food to eat and did all they could to show their appreciation of the music. What a rapid change of fortune within two hours, writes Schehl. Toward noon, riding a good horse, with considerable money in Russian bank notes and a valuable gold watch in his possession, all brought from Moscow, at 1 p.m. he stood dressed in a shirt only, with his bare feet on the frozen ground, and at 2 p. m. he was admired as an artist by a large audience that gave him warm clothes, which meant protection against the danger of freezing to death, and a place near the fire.

During that afternoon and the following night more French soldiers of all arms, mostly emaciated and miserable, were escorted to the camp by Russian militia, peasants, armed with long, sharp lances. It was the night from October 30th to 31st, at the time of the first snowfall, with a temperature of -12 deg. Reaumur (about 5 degrees above zero Fahrenheit). Of the 700 prisoners, many of them deprived of their clothing, as Schehl had been deprived, who had to camp without a fire, quite a number did not see the next morning, and the already described snow hills indicated where these unfortunates had reached the end of their sufferings. The commanding officer of the Cossacks ordered the surviving prisoners to fall in line for the march back to Moscow. The escort consisted of two Cossacks and several hundred peasant-soldiers.

Within sixteen hours the 700 had been reduced to 500. And they had to march back over the road which they had come yesterday as companions of their emperor. The march was slow, they were hardly an hour on the road when here and there one of the poor, half naked, starving men fell into the snow; immediately was he pierced with the lance of one of the peasant soldiers who shouted "*stopai sukinsin*" (forward you dog), but as a rule the one who had fallen was no longer able to obey the brutal command. Two Russian peasant soldiers would then take hold, one at each leg, and drag the dying man with the head over snow and stones until he was dead, then leave the corpse in the middle of the road. In the woods they would practice the same cruelties as the North American Indians, tie those who could not rise to a tree and amuse themselves by torturing the victim to death with their lances. Schehl says:

And I could narrate still other savageries, but they are too revolting, they are worse than those of the savage Indians.

Fortunately, Schehl himself was protected from all molestations by the peasants by the two Cossacks of the escort. He was even taken into the provision wagon where he could ride between bundles of hay and straw. On the evening of the first day's march the troops camped in a birch forest. Russian people are fond of melancholy music; Schehl played for them adagios on his clarinet, and the Cossacks gave him the best they had to eat. His comrades, now reduced to 400 in number, received no food and were so terror-stricken or so feeble that only from time to time they emitted sounds of clamour. Some would crawl into the snow and perish, while those who kept on moving were able to prolong their miserable lives. The second night took away 100 more, so that the number of prisoners was reduced to less than 300 on the morning of October 31st.

During the night from October 31st to November 1st more than one-half of the prisoners who had come into the camp had perished, and there were only about 100 men left to begin the march. This mortality was frightful. Schehl thinks that the peasants killed many during the night in order to be relieved of their guard duty. For the Cossacks would send the superfluous guardsmen away and retain only as many as one for every four prisoners. They saw that the completely exhausted Frenchmen could be driven forward like a herd of sick sheep, and hardly needed any guard. Schehl writes:

In the morning we passed a village in which stood some houses which had not been burned. The returned inhabitants were busy clearing away the rubbish and had built some provisional straw huts. I sat as harmless as possible on my wagon when suddenly a girl in one of the straw huts screamed loud 'Matuschka! Matuschka! Franzusi! Franzusi Niewolni!' (Mother! mother! Frenchmen! French prisoners!), and now sprang forward a large woman, armed with a thick club and struck me such a powerful blow on the head that I became unconscious. When I opened my eyes again the woman struck me once more, this time on my left shoulder and so violently that I screamed. My arm was paralyzed from the stroke. Fortunately, one of the Cossacks came to my rescue, scolded the woman, and chased her away."

On the evening of November 1st, the troops came to a village through which no soldiers had passed, which had not been disturbed by the war. Of the prisoners only sixty remained alive, and these were lodged in the houses.

Schehl describes the interior of the houses of Russian peasants as well as the customs of the Russian peasants, which description is highly interesting, and I shall give a brief abstract of it.

The houses are all frame buildings with a thatched roof, erected upon a foundation of large unhewn stones, the interstices of which are filled with clay, and built in an oblong shape, of strong, round pine logs placed one on top of the other. Each layer is stuffed with moss, and the ends of the logs are interlocking. The buildings consist of one story only, with a very small, unvaulted cellar.

Usually there are only two rooms in these houses, and wealthy peasants use both of them for their personal requirements; the poorer classes, on the other hand, use only one of the rooms for themselves, and the other for their horses, cows, and pigs.

The most prominent part of the interior arrangement of these rooms is the oven, covering about six feet square, with a brick chimney in the houses of the wealthy, but without chimney in those of the poor, so that the smoke must pass through the door giving a varnished appearance to the entire ceiling over the door.

There are no chairs in the rooms; during the day broad benches along the walls and oven are used instead. At night, the members of the household lie down to sleep on these benches, using any convenient piece of clothing for a pillow. It seems the Russian peasant of one hundred years ago considered beds a luxury.

Every one of these houses, those of the rich as well as those of the poor, contains in the easterly corner of the sitting room a cabinet with more or less costly sacred images.

On entering the room the newcomer immediately turns his face toward the cabinet, crossing himself three times in the Greek fashion, simultaneously inclining his head, and not until this act of devotion has been performed does he address individually every one present. In greeting, the family name is never mentioned, only the first name, to which is added: Son of so and so (likewise the first name only), but the inclination of the head—pagoda like—is never omitted.

All the members of the household say their very simple prayers in front of the cabinet; at least, I never heard them say anything else but "*Gospodin pomilui*" (O Lord, have mercy upon us); but such a prayer is very fatiguing for old and feeble persons because *Gospodin pomilui* is repeated at least 24 times, and every repetition is accompanied with a genuflection and a prostration, naturally entailing a great deal of hardship owing to the continued exertion of the entire body.

In addition to the sacred cabinet, the oven, and the benches, every one of the rooms contains another loose bench about six feet long, a table of the same length, and the *kvass* barrel which is indispensable to every Russian.

This cask is a wooden vat of about 50 to 60 gallons capacity, standing upright, the bottom of which is covered with a little rye flour and wheat bran—the poor use chaff of rye—upon which hot water is poured. The water becomes acidulated in about 24 hours and tastes like water mixed with vinegar. A little clean rye straw is placed inside of the vat, in front of the bunghole, allowing the *kvass* to run fairly clear into the wooden cup. When the vat is three-quarters empty more water is added; this must be done very often, as the *kvass* barrel with its single drinking cup—placed always on top of the barrel—is regarded as common property. Every member of the household and every stranger draws and drinks from it to their heart's content, without ever asking permission of the owner of the house.

Kvass is a very refreshing summer drink, especially in the houses of wealthy peasants who need not be particular with their rye flour and who frequently renew the original ingredients of the concoction.

The peasant soldiers took the most comfortable places; for Schehl and his nine comrades, who were lodged with him in one of the houses, straw was given to make a bed on the floor, but most of the nine *syntrophoi* were so sick and feeble that they could not make their couch, and six could not even eat the pound of bread which everyone had received; they hid the remaining bread under the rags which represented their garments. Schehl, although he could not raise his left arm, helped the sick, notwithstanding the pain he suffered, to spread the straw on the floor. On the morning of the 2nd of November the sick, who had not been able to eat all their bread, were dead. Schehl, while the surviving ones were still asleep, took the bread which he found on the corpses, to hide it in his sheepskin coat. This inheritance was to be the means of saving his life; without it he would have starved to death while a prisoner in Moscow.

They left this village with now only twenty-nine prisoners and arrived on the same evening, reduced to eleven in number, in Moscow, where they were locked up in one of the houses, together with many other prisoners. Of the 700 fellow prisoners of Schehl 689 had died during the four days and four nights of hunger, cold, and most barbaric cruelties. If the prisoners had hoped to be saved from further cruelties while in Moscow they were bitterly disappointed. First of all, their guards took from them all they themselves could use, and on this occasion Schehl lost his clarinet which he considered as his life saver. Fortunately, they did not take from him the six pieces of bread. After having been searched the prisoners were driven into a room which was already filled with sick or dying, lying on the floor with very little and bad straw under them. The newcomers had difficulties to find room for themselves among these other unfortunates. The guards brought a pail of fresh water but nothing to eat.

In a room with two windows, which faced the inner courtyard, were locked up over thirty prisoners, and all the other rooms in the building were filled in the same way. During the night from November 2nd to November 3rd several of Schehl's companions died and were thrown through the window into the courtyard, after the jailors had taken from the corpses whatever they could use. Similar acts were performed in the other rooms, and it gave the survivors a little more room to stretch their limbs. This frightful condition lasted six days and six nights, during which time no food was given to them. The corpses in the yard were piled up so high that the pile reached up to the windows.

It was 48 hours since Schehl had eaten the last of the six pieces of bread, and he was so tortured by hunger that he lost all courage, when at 10 o'clock in the forenoon a Russian officer entered and in German ordered the prisoners to get ready within an hour for roll call in the court yard, because the interimistic commanding officer of Moscow, Colonel Orlowski, was to review them. Immediately before this took place, the prisoners had held a counsel among themselves whether it would be wise to offer themselves for Russian military service in order to escape the imminent danger of starving to death. When that officer so unexpectedly had entered, Schehl, although the youngest—he was only 15 years of age—but relatively the strongest, because he was the last of them who had had a little to eat, rose with difficulty from his straw bed and made the offer, saying that they were at present very weak and sick from hunger, but that they would soon regain their strength if they were given something to eat.

The officer in a sarcastic and rough manner replied: "His Majesty our glorious Emperor, Alexander, has soldiers enough and does not need you dogs." He turned and left the room, leaving the unfortunates in a state of despair. Toward 11 o'clock he returned, ordering the prisoners to descend the stairs and fall in line in the court yard. All crawled from their rooms, eighty in number, and stood at attention before the colonel, who was a very handsome and strong man, six foot tall, with expressive and benevolent features. The youth of Schehl made an impression on him, and he asked in German: "My little fellow, are you already a soldier?"

S. At your service, colonel.

C. How old are you?

S. Fifteen years, colonel.

C. How is it possible that you at your young age came into service?

S. Only my passion for horses induced me to volunteer my services in the most beautiful regiment of France, as trumpeter.

C. Can you ride horseback and take care of horses?

S. At your service, colonel!

C. Where are the many prisoners who have been brought here, according to reports there should be 800.

S. What you see here, colonel, is the sad remainder of those 800 men. The others have died.

C. Is there an epidemic disease in this house?

S. Pardon me, colonel, but those comrades of mine have all died from starvation; for during the six days we are here we received no food.

C. What you say, little fellow, cannot be true, for I have ordered to give you the prescribed rations of bread, meat, and brandy, the same as are given to the Russian soldiers, and this has been the will of the *Czar*.

S. Excuse me, colonel, I have told the truth, and if you will take the pains to walk into the rear yard you will see the corpses.

The colonel went and convinced himself of the correctness of my statement. He returned in the greatest anger, addressed some officer in Russian, gave some orders and went along the front to hear Schehl's report confirmed by several other prisoners. The officer who had received orders returned, accompanied by six Uhlans, each of the latter with hazelnut sticks. Now the jailors were called and had to deliver everything which they had taken from their prisoners; unfortunately, Schehl's clarinet was not among the articles that were returned. And now Schehl witnessed the most severe punishment executed on the jailors. They had to remove their coats and were whipped with such cannibal cruelty that bloody pieces of flesh were torn off their backs, and some had to be carried from the place. They deserved severe punishment, for they had sold all the food which during six days had been delivered to them for 800 men.

The surviving prisoners were now treated well, the colonel took Schehl with him to do service in his castle.

The case of Karl Schehl is a typical one.

Holzhausen has collected a great many similar ones from family papers, which never before had been published. All the writers of these papers speak, exactly like Schehl, in plain, truthful language, and the best proof of their veracity is that all, independent of each other, tell the same story of savage cruelty and of robbery. All, in narrating their experiences, do not omit any detail, all give dates and localities which they had retained exactly from those fearful days which had left the most vivid impressions. There is much repetition in these narrations, for all had experienced the same.

All tell that the Cossacks were the first to rob the prisoners. These irregular soldiers received no pay and considered it their right to compensate themselves for the hardships of the campaign by means of robbery.

Besides the tales collected by Holzhausen I can refer to many other writers, Frenchmen, the Englishman Wilson, and even Russians among them, but the material is so voluminous that I shall confine myself to select only what concerned physicians who were taken prisoners.

The Bavarian Sanitary Corps, captured at Polotsk, after having been mercilessly robbed by Cossacks, was brought before a Russian general, who did not even take notice of them. It was only after Russian physicians interfered in their behalf that they obtained a hearing of their grievances.

Prisoners tell touching stories how they were saved by German physicians, in most instances from typhus. In almost all larger Russian cities there were German physicians, and this was a blessing to many of the prisoners. Holzhausen gives the names of several of the sick and the names of the physicians who spared no pains in attending to the sufferers.

In the course of time and with the change of circumstances the lot of the prisoners in general was ameliorated, and in many instances their life became comfortable. Many found employment as farm hands or at some trade, as teachers of languages, but the principal occupation at which they succeeded was the practice of medicine. Whether they were competent physicians or only dilettantes they all gained the confidence of the Russian peasantry. In a land in which physicians are scarce the followers of Aesculap are highly appreciated.

When a Russian peasant had overloaded his stomach and some harmless mixture or decoction given him by some of the pseudo physicians had had a good effect—*post hoc ergo propter hoc*—the medicine man who had come from far away was highly praised and highly recommended.

Lieutenant Furtenbach treated with so-called sympathetic remedies and had a success which surprised nobody more than himself.

Real physicians were appreciated by the educated and influential Russians and secured a more lucrative practice within weeks than they had been able to secure after years at home. Dr. Roos, of whom I have already spoken, having been taken prisoner near the Beresina, became physician to the hospitals of Borisow and Schitzkow and soon had the greatest private practice of any physician in the vicinity; he afterward was called to the large hospitals in St. Petersburg, and was awarded highest honours by the Russian government.

More remarkable was the career of Adjutant Braun which has been told by his friend, Lieutenant Peppler, who acted as his assistant.

Braun had studied medicine for a while, but exchanged sound and lancet for the musket. As prisoner of war, at the urgent request of his friend Peppler, he utilized his unfinished studies. Venaesection was very popular in Russia, he secured a lancet, a German tailor made rollers for him, and soon he shed much Russian blood. The greatest triumph, however, of the two Aesculapians was Braun's successful operation for cataract which he performed on a police officer, his instrument being a rusty needle. The description of the operating scene during which the assistant Peppler trembled from excitement is highly dramatic. Braun became the favourite of the populace and everybody regretted that he left when he was free.

Treatment of Typhus

Among the old publications referring to the medical history of Napoleon's campaign in Russia I found one of a Prussian army physician, Dr. Krantz, published in the year 1817 with the following title: *Bemerkungen ueber den Gang der Krankheiten welche in der königlich preussischen Armee vom Ausbruch des Krieges im Jahre 1812 bis zu Ende des Waffenstillstandes (im Aug.) 1813 geherrscht haben.* (*Remarks on the course of the Diseases which have reigned in the Royal Prussian Army from the Beginning of the War in the Year 1812 until the End of the Armistice [in August] 1813*). From this I shall give the following extract:

It is well known that the soldiers constituting the wreck of the Grand Army wherever they passed on their way from Russia through Germany spread ruin; their presence brought death to thousands of peaceful citizens. Even those who were apparently well carried the germs of disease with them, for we found whole families, says Krantz, in whose dwelling soldiers, showing no signs of disease, had stayed overnight, stricken down with typhus. The Prussian soldiers of York's corps had not been with the Grand Army in Moscow, and there was no typhus among them until they followed the French on their road of retreat from Russia. From this moment on, however, the disease spread with the greatest rapidity in the whole Prussian army corps, and this spreading took place with a certain uniformity among the different divisions.

On account of the overflowing of the rivers, the men had to march closely together on the road, at least until they passed the Vistula near Dirschau, Moeve, and Marienwerder. Of the rapid extent of the infection we can form an idea when we learn the following facts: In the first East Prussian regiment of infantry, when it came to the Vistula, there was not a single case of typhus, while after a march of 14 miles on the highway which the French had passed before them there were

15 to 20 men sick in every company, every tenth or even every seventh man. In those divisions which had been exposed to infection while in former cantonments, the cases were much more numerous, 20 to 30 in every company.

Simultaneously with typhus there appeared the first cases of an epidemic ophthalmy. Although the eye affection was not as general as the typhus—it occurred only in some of the divisions, and then at the outset not so severely as later on—both evils were evidently related to each other by a common causal nexus. They appeared simultaneously under similar circumstances, but never attacked simultaneously the same individual. Whoever had ophthalmy was immune against typhus and vice versa, and this immunity furnished by one against the other evil lasted a long period of time. Both diseases were very often cured on the march. Krantz says:

"We found confirmed what had been asserted a long time before by experienced physicians, that cold air had the most beneficial effect during the inflammatory stage of contagious typhus. For this reason the soldiers who presented the first well-known symptoms of typhus infection: headache, nausea, vertigo, etc., were separated from their healthy comrades and entrusted to medical care, and this consisted, except in the case of extraordinarily grave symptoms, in dressing the patient with warm clothing and placing him for the march on a wagon where he was covered all over with straw.

The wagon was driven fast, to follow the corps, but halted frequently on the way at houses where tea (*Infusum Chamomillae, species aromaticarum*, etc.) with or without wine or *spiritus sulphuricus aetherius* were prepared; of this drink the patient was given a few cupfuls to warm him. As a precaution against frost, which proved to be a very wise one, hands and feet were wrapped in rags soaked in *spiritus vini camphoratus*. For quarters at night isolated houses were selected for their reception—a precaution taught by sad experience—and surgeons or couriers who had come there in advance had made the best preparations possible.

All the hospitals between the Vistula and Berlin, constantly overfilled, were thoroughly infected, and thus transformed into regular pest-houses exhaling perdition to everyone who entered, the physicians and attendants included. On the other hand, most of the patients who were treated on the march recovered. Of 31 cases of typhus of the 2nd battalion of the infantry guards transported from Tilsit to Tuchel, only one died, while the remaining 30 regained their health completely, a statistical result as favourable as has hardly ever happened in the best regulated hospital and which is the more surprising on account of the severe form of the disease at that time.

An equally favourable result was obtained in the first East Prussian regiment of infantry on the march from the Vistula to the Spree. There was not a single death on the march; of 330 patients 300 recovered, 30 were sent into hospitals of Elbing, Maerkisch Friedland, Conitz, and Berlin, and the same excellent results were reported from other divisions of the corps where the same method had been followed.

A most remarkable observation among the immense number of patients was that they seldom presented a stage of convalescence. Three days after they had been free from fever for 24 hours they were fit, without baggage, for a half or even a whole day's march. If the recovery had not been such a speedy one, how could all the wagons have been secured in that part of the country devastated by war for the transportation of the many hundreds of sick.

At the beginning of the sickness a *vomitium* of *ipecacuanha* and *tartarus* stibiatus was administered (though on the march no real medical treatment was attempted); later on *aether vitrioli* with *tinctura valerianae, tinctura aromatica* and finally *tinctura chinae composita* aurantiorum with good wine, etc., were given. It is interesting to read Krantz's statement of how much some physicians were surprised who had been accustomed to treat their patients in hospitals according to the principles of that period, which consisted in the exclusion of fresh air and the hourly administration of medicine. The mortality of those treated on the march in the manner described was never more than 2 to 3 *per cent.*

As already mentioned, an epidemic ophthalmy spread simultaneously with typhus among a large number of the troops returning from Courland, especially among those who formed the rear guard, in which was the first East Prussian regiment to which Krantz was attached.

In a far greater proportion the men of the two Prussian cavalry regiments and artillery batteries which Napoleon had taken with him to Moscow, that is into ruin, succumbed to the morbid potencies which acted upon them from all sides.

On March 17th, 1813, York's corps entered Berlin, and from this time on contagious typhus disappeared almost completely in this army division. It is true that occasionally a soldier was attacked, but the number of these was insignificant, and the character of the sickness was mild. Other internal diseases were also infrequent among these troops during that time. Epidemic ophthalmy, however, was very prevalent in the East Prussian regiment of infantry. From February, 1813, until the day of the Battle of Leipzig, 700 men were treated for this disease. The character of this ophthalmy was mild, and under treatment the patients completely recovered within a few days (nine days at most) without any destructive lesion remaining. Quite different from this form was a severe ophthalmy which appeared in the army toward the end of the year 1813, and also during the years 1814 and 1815.

After the Second Crossing of the Niemen

Out of the enemy's country, on their way home, the soldiers had by no means reached the limit of their sufferings. Instead of being able now to take the much longed for and so much needed rest they were compelled to keep on marching in order to reach the meeting places designated to them, the principal one of which was Koenigsberg.

Before entering Prussia they had to pass through a district which was inhabited by Lithuanians who had suffered very much from the army passing on the march to Moscow, and who now took revenge on the retreating soldiers.

Most happy were the Germans of the army breathing again the air of their native country, and they could not restrain their feelings when they found themselves in clean dwellings.

Their first occupation was to restore themselves in regard to cleanliness, to free their faces from a thick covering of dirt intensified by smoke which could be compared with a mask. All these unfortunate men wore this mask, but, as they said while in Moscow, without any desire to dance. Especially the better educated ones among them felt ashamed to present themselves in this condition in which they had dragged themselves through Russia and Poland.

On December 16th, von Borcke and his General, von Ochs, came to Schirwind, for the first time again in a Prussian city. Quarters were assigned to them in one of the best houses, the house of the widow of a Prussian officer. The lady, on seeing the two entering the house, was astonished to learn that they were a general with his adjutant, and that they should be her guests. Nothing about them indicated their rank, they were wrapped in sheepskins and rags full of dirt, blackened by the smoke from the camp fires, with long beards, frozen hands and feet.

On January 2nd., 1813, these two officers arrived at Thorn. They considered themselves saved from the great catastrophe, when there, like in all places to which the wrecks of the grand army had come, typhus broke out. General von Ochs was stricken down with this disease, and his condition did not warrant any hopes for recovery. His son, however, who had gone through the whole retreat wounded and sick with typhus, whom the general and his adjutant had brought from Borodino in a wagon under incredible difficulties, had recovered and was able to nurse his father.

And General von Ochs came home with his Adjutant, von Borcke, on February 20th, 1813.

Good people took pains to give their guests an opportunity to clean themselves thoroughly; the well-to-do had their servants attend to this process; in houses of the working class man and wife would give a helping hand.

Sergeant Schoebel, together with a comrade, was quartered in the house of an honest tailor who, seeing how the soldiers were covered with lice, made them undress and, while the wife boiled the undergarments, the tailor ironed the outer clothing with a hot iron.

Generous people tried to ameliorate in every manner possible the need which presented itself in such a pitiful form.

Lieutenant Schauroth was sitting in despair at a table in an inn when one nobleman pressed a double *Louisd'or* into his hand and another placed his sleigh at the lieutenant's disposal to continue his journey.

In Tapiau a carpenter's helper, himself a very poor man, begged among his friends to obtain a suit of clothes for Sergeant Steinmueller, whom he had never known before.

But cases of this kind were the exception; in general the Prussian peasants remembered the many excesses which, notwithstanding Napoleon's strict orders, the soldiers had committed on their march through East Prussia; they remembered the requisitions, they felt the plight of Prussia since the Battle of Jena, and they revenged themselves on the French especially, but even the Germans of Napoleon's soldiers had to suffer from the infuriated, pitiless peasantry. Holzhausen describes scenes which were not less atrocious than those enacted by Russian peasants.

And those who were treated kindly had the most serious difficulties: the sudden change from misery to regular life caused many serious disorders of the organs of digestion, enervation and circulation.

All who have been in the field during our civil war know how long it took before they were able again to sleep in a bed. The Napoleonic soldiery describe how the warmth of the bed brought on the most frightful mental pictures; they saw burnt, frozen, and mutilated comrades and had to try to find rest on the floor, their nervous and their circulatory systems were excited to an intolerable degree. After eating they vomited, and only gradually the ruined stomach became accustomed again, first, to thin soups and, later on, to a more substantial diet.

How much they had suffered manifested itself in many ways after the thick crust had been removed from their body and, above all, after what had taken the place of shoes had been taken off. When Sergeant Toenges removed the rags from his feet the flesh of both big toes came off. Captain Gravenreuth's boots had been penetrated by matter and ichor. Painful operations had to be performed to separate gangrenous parts. In Marienwerder Hochberg found all the attendants of Marshal Victor on the floor while a surgeon was amputating their limbs.

But these were comparatively minor affairs, amputated limbs played no role when hundreds of thousands of mutilated corpses rested on the fields of Russia.

An enemy more vicious than the one that had decimated the beautiful army was lying in wait for the last remainder which tried to rally again.

It was the typhus that on the road from Moscow all through Germany and through France did its destructive work.

This disease had been observed, as Dr. Geissler reports, first in Moscow, ravaged most terribly in Wilna and held a second great harvest in Koenigsberg, where the first troops arrived on December 20th.

One-half of those who had been attacked succumbed, although the hospitals of Koenigsberg were ideal ones compared with those of Wilna.

Geissler and his colleague had to work beyond description to ameliorate and to console; help was impossible in the majority of cases.

The physicians of Koenigsberg were not as lucky as Dr. Krantz, whose patients were in the open air instead of being confined in a hospital.

It is heartrending to read how so many who had withstood so much, escaped so many dangers, had to die now. One of these was General Eblé, the hero of the Beresina.

144

CARTE FIGURATIVE des pertes successives en hommes de l'Armée Française dans la campagne de Russie 1812-1813.

Dressée par M.Minard, Inspecteur Général des Ponts et Chaussées en retraite.

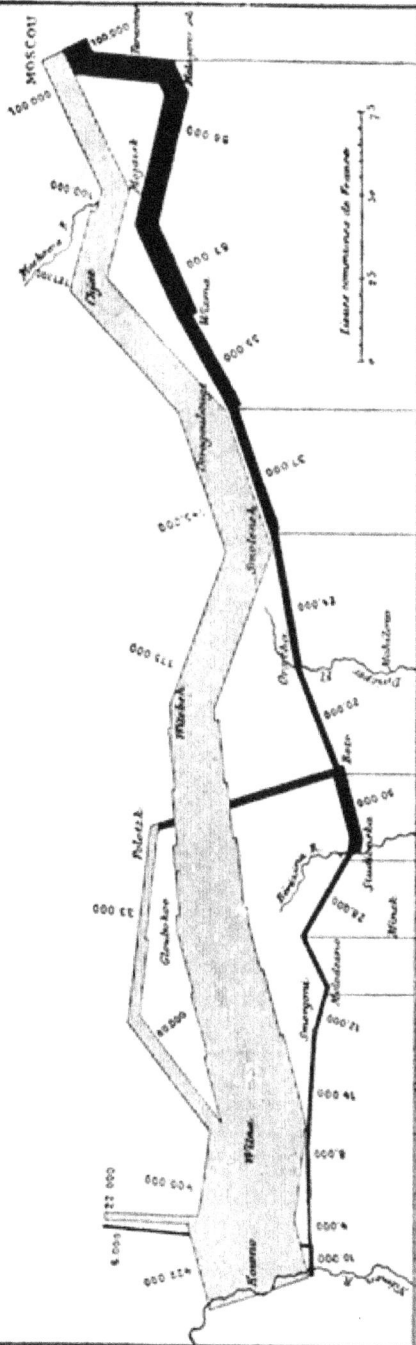

MOSCOU

100.000

100.000

96.000

100.000

127.100

87.000

55.000

Tarantino

Malo-Jaroslaveiz

Wixma

Dorogobouge

37.000

Mojaisk

Gjate

24.000

Smolensk

175.000

Orscha

22.000

Witebsk

Bobr

20.000

Mohilow

Dnieper

Polotzk

90.000

6.000

33.000

Studienska

Bérésina R.

24.000

Glouboko

96.000

Minsk

12.000

Smorgoni

14.000

Moiodezno

8.000

Wilna

122.000

Kowno

4.000

6.000

4.000

10.000

Niémen

28.000

175.000

37.000

Lieues communes de France

0   25   50   75

TABLEAU GRAPHIQUE de la température en degrés du thermomètre de Réaumur au dessous de zero

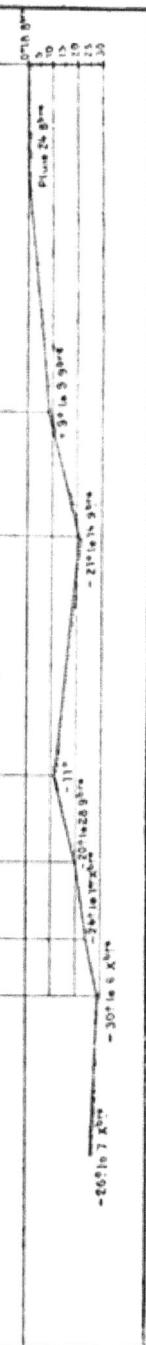

Pluie 24 8bre

0° 18 8bre

— 9° le 9 9bre

zéro

— 11°

— 21° le 14 9bre

— 20° le 28 9bre

— 24° le 1er 9bre

— 30° le 6 Xbre

— 26° le 7 Xbre

0°
5
10
15
20
25
30

www.ingramcontent.com/pod-product-compliance
Lightning Source LLC
Chambersburg PA
CBHW021006090426
42738CB00007B/679